Oxford French Cartoon-strip Vocabulary Builder

With illustrations by Claire Bretécher
Edited by Marie-Hélène Corréard

OXFORD
UNIVERSITY PRESS

OXFORD
UNIVERSITY PRESS

Great Clarendon Street, Oxford OX2 6DP

Oxford University Press is a department of the University of Oxford.
It furthers the University's objective of excellence in research, scholarship,
and education by publishing worldwide in

Oxford New York

Athens Auckland Bangkok Bogotá Buenos Aires Calcutta
Cape Town Chennai Dar es Salaam Delhi Florence Hong Kong Istanbul
Karachi Kuala Lumpur Madrid Melbourne Mexico City Mumbai
Nairobi Paris São Paulo Singapore Taipei Tokyo Toronto Warsaw

with associated companies in Berlin Ibadan

Oxford is a registered trade mark of Oxford University Press
in the UK and in certain other countries

Published in the United States
by Oxford University Press Inc., New York

English and French text © Oxford University Press 2000
Illustrations © Claire Bretécher

British Library Cataloguing in Publication Data

Data available

Library of Congress Cataloging in Publication Data

Data available

ISBN 0–19–860267–7

3 5 7 9 10 8 6 4 2

Typeset by Fine Print in Kosmik
Printed in Italy by Giunti

Contents

Introduction		page 5
How to use the book		6
List of abbreviations		6
Guide to pronunciation		7

Story:	Topic:	
Moi	Describing people	8-9
Célébrité en ligne	Greetings	10-11
Ménage	Going out	12-13
La vie	Education	14-15
Yellow Submarine	Family	16-17
La crise	Home	18-19
Loisirs	Pastimes	20-21
Communication	Communication	22-23
Mots et mode	Approval and disapproval	24-25
Complainte	Dates	26-27
Challenge	Travelling	28-29
Pourboire	Money	30-31
L'amitié	Love and relationships	32-33
Invasion	On the phone	34-35
Au bercail	Time off	36-37
Le cerveau	Computing and the Internet	38-39
Soucis	Emotions	40-41
Le boulet	Food and drink	42-43
Anniversaire	Art and literature	44-45
Bavure	The Earth	46-47
Karma	Health	48-49
Photo	Clothes	50-51
Top 50	Television	52-53
Pense à ton avenir	Work	54-55
Projets d'avenir	The human body	56-57
Barbecue	Transport	58-59
Sports	Sport	60-61
Sur écoute	Economy	62-63
Littérature	Numbers	64-65
Renaissance	Religion and beliefs	66-67

Glossary	68-73
Verbs	74-80

Proprietary terms

Credits and acknowledgements

Editor **Marie-Hélène Corréard**
Cartoons by **Claire Bretécher**

I would like to thank **Mary O'Neill** for the Guide to Pronunciation and **Janet King** who was my consultant for English language.

M.H.C.

Introduction

Anyone learning a foreign language wants to be able to speak it as it is really spoken. This book will help you achieve this. Most coursebooks tend to reflect "standard" language—the language you hear on the radio or television or in formal contexts. This book covers the language of everyday, informal social situations.

A text written only in "spoken language" looks odd. Situations which are perfectly clear in conversation are not so easy to understand when reduced to dialogues on a page. Tapes and videos require special equipment. Cartoon strips overcome these difficulties and are an ideal vehicle for the efficient learning of spoken language. The characters feel real and their roles are very clear. The situations are immediately accessible and do not need to be described at length. Added to which, in France cartoons are extremely popular and enjoyed by adults and teenagers alike. Claire Bretécher's cartoons are no exception; they are well known and loved.

Spoken language is different from standard language for several reasons. It uses words which rarely appear in written form except in dictionaries (**môme** instead of **enfant**). Some grammatical rules which are strictly applied when writing are often ignored when speaking, in particular negative forms are simplified (**je sais pas** instead of **je ne sais pas**). Abbreviated forms of words are used more freely (**à plute** or **à plus** instead of **à plus tard**).

This book is based on Claire Bretécher's Agrippine's series. The texts have been adapted to be suitable for learners and each one introduces a theme developed in the material which accompanies each story.

A more detailed description of all the sections of the book is given in **How to use the book**.

The stories help learners to memorize themes and new words, and vocabulary learning becomes an enjoyable and rewarding experience.

How to use the book

The French Cartoon-strip Vocabulary Builder is designed to make vocabulary learning both efficient and enjoyable. It is built around thirty cartoon strips and themes, each presented on a double-page spread, with a clear emphasis on spoken language.

Each story is supplemented by three sections:

1. Understanding the text

This lists all the key words used in the cartoon strip on the facing page and gives grammatical information as well as contextual translations.

2. Key Structures

This section lists and explains phrases which are hard to understand even if all the individual constituents are known. It also supplies information on those phrases commonly used in spoken language that will be useful for a learner.

3. Vocabulary

This section groups together the essential words and phrases from the vocabulary-building topic introduced in the story. Grammatical information (gender for nouns, feminine forms for adjectives and nouns) is also supplied.

Additional notes in text bubbles explain culture-specific references appearing in the text.

French verbs are usually followed by a number. This number refers to the conjugation pattern shown in the conjugation table at the end of the book.

For easy access, the topics are listed in the table of **contents**.

The **glossary** at the end of the book lists all the words that appear in the stories and their translations with the relevant page number(s). Informal words used only in spoken language are clearly marked with the symbol ⓖ.

Advice on pronunciation rules and sounds in French is given in the **Guide to pronunciation**.

List of abbreviations

adj	adjective
adj inv	invariable adjective
adv	adverb
conj	conjunction
det	determiner
excl	exclamation
nf	feminine noun
nfpl	plural feminine noun
nm	masculine noun
nm/f	masculine/feminine noun
nmf	masculine or feminine noun
nmpl	plural masculine noun
nprf	feminine proper noun
nprm	masculine proper noun
prep	preposition
pron	pronoun
v	verb
ⓖ	WARNING: this symbol indicates that a word is used only in spoken language
→	see

Guide to pronunciation

The table below was designed to help English speakers bridge the gap between the sound systems of English and French. It aims to connect French sounds to their possible written representations, illustrating the link by means of examples.

In many cases, the sounds are similar, if not actually the same. In others, it is only possible to give an approximation of the French sound by using English sounds. This is particularly true of the French vowels which are nasalized [ɛ̃], [ɑ̃], [ɔ̃], [œ̃] and those which require a marked degree of lip rounding [ø], [œ], [y], [ɥ].

phonetic symbol	sounds like	written in French like	examples
[a]	cat, flat	a, à, ha–	acheter, bagarre, **à**, voil**à**, hasard (**note also** fe**mm**e)
[ɑ]	arm, car	â, a	âgé, Pâques, bas
[e]	hay, tray but shorter	–er, –es, –ez, –é(e), é	aller, des, nez, cassé, année, étage
[ɛ]	pet, threat	–è–, ê, e, ai, –ais, ei–, aî–, –è–	frère, même, être, cet, elle, aime, anglais, peine, connaître Noèl
[i]	treat, fleet	i, –ie, –î–, hi–, y, –ys, ï	fille, pile, vie, pris, illisible, bîbîp, y, hibou, pays, haïr
[o]	show, toe	au, aud, eau, aux, eaux, o, ô	aussi, chaud, beau, château, journaux, eaux, chose, trop, gros, obligatoire, côte, môme
[ɔ]	hot, what	o–, ho–, hô–	opérer, donner, horreur
[u]	hoot, flute	ou, où, –oû–, –oo–, hou–, –oux, –oue	oublier, fou, mourir, amour, où, août, football, houx, roux, roue
[ə]	ago, gather (in British English)	e (silent at the end of words and may even be left out)	mère, elle, j'aime, même, premier, menu, l(e), n(e), d(e), p(le)tit, f(e)ra
[ø]	~ purr, her but shorter	eu, eux	peu, neveu, bleu, heureuse, heureux, cheveux, yeux
[oe]	~ as above but longer	eu, œu–, heu–, œ	peur, déjeuner, horreur, fauteuil, sœur, heure, œil
[y]	ee but with rounded lips	u, û, hu	une, rue, vendu, eu, sûr, humeur
[ɛ̃]	an / am + nasal twang	in, im, ain, –ein, –yn, –en, –aim, hein	intention, matin, imbécile, copain, plein, déteindre, sympa, rien,
[ɑ̃]	awn / alm+ nasal twang	an, en–, em, –ent, am	an, andouille, entrer, ennuyer, emmener, temps, souvent
[ɔ̃]	on + nasal twang	on, –hon–, om	onze, bon, monter, honte, compter, se tromper
[œ̃]	fun, son + nasal twang	–un –um	un, brun, lundi
[j]	yes, player	–i–, y, –il, –lle, –ll–	bien, ciel, payer, travail, feuille, fille
[w]	~ was	oi, –oî–, ou, –	oiseau, voir, quoi, oui, boîte,
[ɥ]	~ we, tweet	–ui–, hui, –uî–	nuit, lui, aujourd'hui, huit
[b]	as English	b, –bb–	béton, biberon, abbaye
[d]	– " –	d, –dd–	devoir, aide, addition
[f]	– " –	f, –ff–, ph	fête, affaires, neuf, téléphone, photo
[k]	– " –	c, qu, –q, –cc–, k–,–ck–, –ch–	café, sac, quand, quoi, coq, occupé, kilo, orchestre, ticket
[l]	– " –	l, –ll–	lettre, pile, ville, salle
[m]	– " –	m, –mm–	mère, nombre, femme
[n]	– " –	n, –nn–	non, animal, panne, donner
[p]	– " –	p, –pp–, –bs–	pomme, chapeau, appuyer, hop, observer
[s]	– " –	s, –ss–, c, ç, sc–, –x	son, festival, asseoir, poisson, cette, cinéma, garçon, ça, reçu, scène, piscine, six, saucisson
[t]	– " –	t, –tt–, th	tapis, auto, thé, sympathique
[v]	– " –	v, w	venir, lever, grave, wagon, W–C
[z]	– " –	s, z, –x–	maison, loisirs, zoo, amazonienne, dix-huit, sixième
[g]	– " –	g, gu–, –gg–	gamin, garage, guitare, agresser
[ʒ]	leisure, seizure	j, g	j'ai, jeune, déjeuner, plage, gifle, mangeons, giga, génial
[ʃ]	rash, shoe	ch, sh	chinois, acheter, short
[ɲ]	new, onion	gn	ignorer, soigner, champignon
[ŋ]	sing, wrong	–ng	camping, parking
[r]	~ a very soft loch sound produced at the back of the throat	r, –rr–, rh	rouge, partir, arrêter, serrurerie

MOI

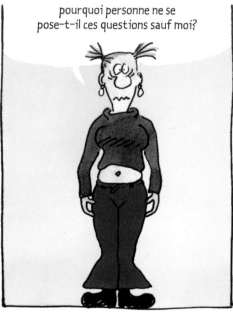

Understanding the text

autre (adj)	other
ce/cette (adj)	this
écouter (v[1])	to listen to
enfermé/enfermée (adj)	locked in
envoyer (v[2])	to send
être (v[3])	to be
exister (v[1])	to exist
moi (pron)	me
moi-même (pron)	myself
moins (adv)	less
parler (v[1])	to talk
personne (pron)	nobody
poser (v[1]) **une question**	to ask a question
pourquoi (adv)	why
quelque part	somewhere
une **question** (nf)	question
qui (pron)	who
une **salle de bains** (nf)	bathroom

sauf (prep)	except
se sentir (v[4])	to feel
seul/seule (adj)	only
si (conj)	if
un **signal** (nm)	sign
toi (pron)	you

⇥ Key Structures

qui es-tu?	who are you?
est-ce moi?	is it me?
poser une question	to ask a question
se poser une question	to ask oneself a question
un seul signal	only one sign

⇥ Describing People

my name is Agrippine	je m'appelle Agrippine
I'm 16 years old	j'ai 16 ans
I'm 1.68 m tall	je mesure 1,68 m
I weigh 55 kilos	je pèse 55 kilos
my hair is blond	j'ai les cheveux blonds
his eyes are blue	il a les yeux bleus
I live in a house	j'habite dans une maison
my room is on the first floor	ma chambre est au premier étage
she's a student	elle est étudiante
I like to read and to ski	j'aime lire et faire du ski
I hate music	je déteste la musique
I often go to the cinema	je vais souvent au cinéma
I take guitar lessons	je prends des cours de guitare
pleasant	agréable
ambitious	ambitieux/ambitieuse
funny	drôle
to be in a good mood	être de bonne humeur
to be in a bad mood	être de mauvaise humeur
intelligent	intelligent/intelligente
polite	poli/polie
lazy	paresseux/paresseuse
patient	patient/patiente
nice	sympa
shy	timide
tall	grand/grande
big	gros/grosse
ugly	laid/laide
good-looking	beau/belle
slim	mince
thin	maigre
old	vieux/vieille
her hair is long	elle a les cheveux longs
he wears glasses	il porte des lunettes
he shaved his moustache	il s'est coupé la moustache
he is growing a beard	il se laisse pousser la barbe
curly hair	des cheveux bouclés
straight hair	des cheveux raides
I prefer short hair	je préfère les cheveux courts

CÉLÉBRITÉ EN LIGNE

Understanding the text

alors (adv)	then
un **appel** (nm)	phone call
un **arrêt** (nm)	stop
sans **arrêt**	non-stop
attendre (v[6])	to wait
aussi (adv)	also
la **beauté** (nf)	beauty
ben (excl)	h'm
bloquer (v[1])	to block
un **bouton** (nm)	button
une **célébrité** (nf)	celebrity
une **communication** (nf)	call
un **coup de fil** (nm)	phone call
demander (v[1])	to ask
écouter (v[1])	to listen
un **espace** (nm)	complex
éviter (v[1])	to avoid
faire (v[5])	to do
faux/fausse (adj)	wrong
une **faveur** (nf)	favour
un **garage** (nm)	garage
grave (adj)	serious
un **hasard** (nm)	chance
par hasard	by chance
important/importante (adj)	important
une **ligne** (nf)	line
en ligne	on line
un **monde** (nm)	people
tout le monde	everybody
neuf/neuve (adj)	new
un **numéro** (nm)	number
obligé/obligée (adj)	obliged
une **occasion** (nf)	second-hand car
un **ourlet** (nm)	hem
passer (v[1])	to put through
une **pièce** (nf)	part
une **pièce détachée** (nf)	spare part
pouvoir (v[7])	to be able to, can
prendre (v[8])	to take
un **pressing** (nm)	dry-cleaner's
regretter (v[1])	to regret
salut (excl)	bye
une **serrurerie** (nf)	locksmith's
sonner (v[1])	to ring
une **transformation** (nf)	alteration
se tromper (v[1])	to make a mistake
trop (adv)	too much

Greetings

Meetings	Rencontres
good morning	bonjour
good afternoon	bonjour
good evening	bonsoir
hello	salut
how are you?	comment-allez vous?
how are things?	ça va?
how nice to see you	ça me fait plaisir de vous voir
long time, no see	il y a longtemps que nous ne nous sommes pas vus
let me introduce my brother	permettez-moi de vous présenter mon frère
this is Jean-Mathieu	je vous présente Jean-Mathieu
pleased to meet you	enchanté de faire votre connaissance

Partings	Séparations
goodbye	au revoir
bye	salut
see you	à plus tard, (more colloquial) à plus
have a good day	bonne journée
have a good evening	bonne fin de journée
have a good night	bonne nuit

Key Structures

dis donc	hey
ça sonne	it's ringing
être en train de + infinitive	
elle est en train de travailler	she's working
tu n'es pas en train de prendre mes appels pour éviter que je ne te bloque la ligne?	you're not taking my calls so that I don't block the line by any chance?
elle s'est trompée de numéro	she got the wrong number
être obligé à quelqu'un de + infinitive	
je te serais obligée de me passer mes communications	I'd be obliged if you transferred my calls

MÉNAGE

Understanding the text

alors (adv)	then
appeler (v[9])	to call
après (adv)	afterwards
arriver (v[1])	to arrive
avant (prep)	before
avoir (v[10])	to have
une **bagarre** (nf)	fight
beaucoup (adv)	a lot
boire (v[11])	to drink
bu	→ **boire**
une **carte d'identité** (nf)	identity card
une **casserole** (nf)	saucepan
une **chaîne** (nf)	chain
faire (v[5]) **la chaîne**	to make a chain
chez (prep)	at
coincer ⓖ (v[12])	to catch
un/une **copain/copine** (nm/f)	boyfriend/girlfriend
déteindre (v[13])	to run
dire à (v[14])	to tell
embarquer ⓖ (v[1])	to pick up
embrasser (v[1])	to kiss
un **feu** (nm)	fire
finalement (adv)	finally
un **flic** ⓖ (nm)	cop
un **goinfre** (nm)	greedy pig
une **grenade lacrymogène** (nf)	tear gas grenade
il y a eu	there was
imaginer (v[1])	to imagine
un **journal** (nm)	a paper
journaux (nmpl)	→ **journal**
une **lampe halogène** (nf)	halogen lamp
une **larme** (nf)	tear
être en larmes	to be in tears
manger (v[15])	to eat
le **ménage** (nm)	housework
mettre (v[24]) **le feu à**	to set fire to
nous (pron)	us
parce que (conj)	because
parents (nmpl)	parents
partir (v[4])	to leave
un **père** (nm)	father
personne (pron)	nobody
plus (adv)	more
pourquoi (adv)	why
prévoir (v[16])	to plan
quelqu'un (pron)	somebody
ranger (v[15])	to tidy up
rentrer (v[1])	to come home
renverser (v[1])	to knock over
réviser (v[1])	to revise
sauf (prep)	except
savoir (v[17])	to know
une **scène** (nf)	scene
une **soirée** (nf)	party
se suicider (v[1])	to commit suicide
un **tapis** (nm)	rug
terrible (adj)	dreadful
tôt (adv)	early
tout le monde	everybody
venir (v[18])	to come
vouloir (v[19])	to want

⊡ Going Out

entertainment	le spectacle
a disco	une boîte de nuit
a nightclub	une boîte de nuit
a theatre	un théâtre
a play	une pièce
a comedy	une comédie
an opera	un opéra
an opera house	un opéra
a ballet	un ballet
a concert	un concert
classical music	la musique classique
a film, a movie	un film
a documentary film	un documentaire
a party	une fête
dinner in a restaurant	un dîner au restaurant
an evening with friends	une soirée chez des copains
to have a celebration	faire une fête
to go out	sortir

S.O.S. Médecins is an emergency doctor service that responds to home calls.

In France **la carte d'identité** is an official document that provides proof of identity and nationality.

⊡ Key Structures

il faut + infinitive	
il faut réserver sa place à l'avance	you have to book your seat in advance
il a fallu appeler les parents de Sébastien	we had to call Sebastien's parents
il nous a fait ranger	he made us tidy up

LA VIE

Understanding the text

aller (v[25])	→ Key Structures
un **amant** (nm)	lover
un **amour** (nm)	love
s'**amuser** (v[1])	to enjoy oneself
l' **avenir** (nm)	future
le **bien** (nm)	good
faire (v[5]) **du bien**	to do good
bon (adv)	right
un **boulet** (nm)	millstone
cesser (v[1])	to stop
dire (v[14])	to say
un **échec** (nm)	failure
un **effort** (nm)	effort
un/une **enfant** (nmf)	child
s'**ennuyer** (v[20])	to be bored
être (v[3])	to be
faire (v[5])	to make
une **fesse** (nf)	buttock
un **fossoyeur** (nm)	gravedigger
horrible (adj)	horrid
jamais (adv)	never
jeune (adj)	young
la **jeunesse** (nf)	youth
un **leurre** (nm)	illusion
mignon/mignonne (adj)	cute
le **monde** (nm)	world
mourir (v[21])	to die
la **peur** (nf)	fear
avoir peur	to be scared
se **remuscler** (v[1])	to become muscular again
rencontrer (v[1])	to meet
seul/seule (adj)	on one's own
un **sujet** (nm)	subject
au sujet de	about
un **tas** ⊚ (nm)	heap
des tas ⊚ **de**	lots of
tout (adj)	any
travailler (v[1])	to work
vide (adj)	empty
une **vie** (nf)	life
vivre (v[22])	to live
voir (v[23])	to see
voué/vouée à l'échec (adj)	doomed to failure
un **voyage** (nm)	journey

Education

a class	**une classe**
a classroom	**une salle de classe**
a pupil	**un/une écolier/écolière**
a student	**un/une élève**
a university student	**un/une étudiant/étudiante**
the curriculum	**le programme**
an exam	**un examen**
to take an exam	**passer un examen**
to pass an exam	**réussir un examen**
faire des études	**to be a student**
faire des études de droit	**to study law**
a PhD	**un doctorat**

The French school system:
l'école maternelle, for children aged 2 to 6;
l'école primaire, for children aged 7 to 11;
le collège, for children aged 12 to 15;
le lycée for students aged 16 to 18.

la rentrée refers to the period after the summer break when students go back to school/university (from September to October).

Key Structures

qu'est-ce qu'il y a?	what's the matter?

aller + infinitive is used to express the future tense

il va être furieux	he's going to be furious
je vais leur dire	I'll tell them
tu vas t'amuser	you'll have fun
tu vas travailler	you'll have a job
faire des voyages	to travel
faire du bien	to do good
on ne cesse de s'ennuyer que pour avoir peur	you stop being bored only to become scared
ça me fait du bien ce que tu dis	what you're saying does me good

YELLOW SUBMARINE

Understanding the text

à côté de (prep)	next to
l'anglais (nm)	English language
aura	→ **avoir**
avoir (v[10])	to have
ça craint	it's the pits
une **cassette** (nf)	cassette
chanter (v[1])	to sing
complètement (adv)	completely
connaître (v[30])	to know
un **cours** (nm)	class
demain (adv)	tomorrow
un **devoir** (nm)	essay
être (v[3])	to be
faux (adv)	out of tune
une **gifle** (nf)	slap in the face
s'inquiéter (v[26])	to worry
lire (v[27])	to read
le **matin** (nm)	morning
moi (pron)	me
moi non plus	me neither
on (pron)	we
oublier (v[28])	to forget
une **parole** (nf)	word
pour (prep)	for
puer (v[1])	to stink
quand (conj)	when
quoi (pron)	what
sur (prep)	about
se taire (v[29])	to be quiet
tais-toi	→ **se taire**
toi (pron)	you

→ Family

a father	**un père**
a mother	**une mère**
a grandfather	**un grand-père**
a grandmother	**une grand-mère**
a brother	**un frère**
a sister	**une sœur**
a son	**un fils**
a daughter	**une fille**
an uncle	**un oncle**
an aunt	**une tante**
a great uncle	**un grand-oncle**
a great aunt	**une grande-tante**
a nephew	**un neveu**
a niece	**une nièce**
a father-in-law	**un beau-père**
a mother-in-law	**une belle-mère**
a son-in-law	**un gendre**
a daughter-in-law	**une bru**
a brother-in-law	**un beau-frère**
a sister-in-law	**une belle-sœur**
a cousin	**un cousin/une cousine**
a stepfather	**un beau-père**
a stepmother	**une belle-mère**
a stepbrother	**un demi-frère**
a stepsister	**une demi-sœur**
a relation	**un parent**
relations	**la famille**
parents	**les parents**
to get married	**se marier** [28]
to marry somebody	**se marier avec quelqu'un**
to live together	**vivre ensemble**
to divorce	**divorcer** [12]
to split up	**se séparer** [1]

→ Key Structures

The imperative mood is used to give orders:

chante!	sing!
tais-toi!	be quiet!
ne t'inquiète pas!	don't worry!

LA CRISE

Understanding the text

à peu près (adv)	about
acheter (v[31])	to buy
une année (nf)	year
aujourd'hui (adv)	today
avoir (v[10])	to have
baisser (v[1])	to go down
bon (adv)	right
une cervelle (nf)	brain
combien de (det)	how many
comment (adv)	how
comment ça	how
continuer (v[1])	to continue
cosmique (adj)	cosmic
une crise (nf)	crisis
dégringoler (v[1])	to slump
dernier/dernière (adj)	last
deviner (v[1])	to guess
dire (v[14])	to say
s'embrasser (v[1])	to kiss (one another)
emménager (v[15])	to move in
il y a	there is
un lave-vaisselle (nm)	dishwasher
un lycée (nm)	secondary school (15–18)
un m² (nm)	m², square metre
une marque (nf)	make
une mère (nf)	mother
une moitié (nf)	half
un nom (nm)	name
un oiseau (nm)	bird
un oncle (nm)	uncle
parfaitement (adv)	absolutely
payer (v[32])	to pay
pourtant (adv)	and yet
prendre (v[8])	to take
près de (prep)	near
un prix (nm)	price
rompre (v[33])	to break up
savoir (v[17])	to know
un studio (nm)	studio flat, studio apartment
des travaux (nmpl)	work
trouver (v[1])	to find
tuer (v[1])	to kill
voir (v[23])	to see

Figures in French are set out differently:
where English would have a comma, French simply
has a space (or sometimes a full stop/period).
450 000 francs 450,000 francs
French uses a comma where English has a decimal point.
19,95 francs 19.95 francs

The size of flats and houses is given in **mètres carrés**
(square metres) **30 m²**

➡ Key Structures

combien?	how much?
combien coûte ta maison?	how much does your house cost?
combien de...	how many...
combien de pièces?	how many rooms?
c'est cosmique ce que les prix ont baissé	it's incredible how much prices have gone down
c'est étonnant ce que...	it's amazing how much...
l'année dernière	last year
à moitié prix	at half price

➡ Home

a flat, an apartment	**un appartement**
a house	**une maison individuelle**
a co-owner	**un/une copropriétaire**
a tenant	**un/une locataire**
to rent a house	**louer une maison**
to let a house	**louer une maison**
to live in the country	**habiter à la campagne**
the city centre	**le centre ville**
the suburbs	**la banlieue**
a block of flats	**un immeuble d'habitation**
a 1-bedroom flat	**un deux pièces cuisine**
a studio flat	**un studio**
a bedroom with a sea view	**une chambre avec vue sur la mer**
an equipped kitchen	**une cuisine équipée**
a bedroom	**une chambre**
a room	**une pièce**
a lounge	**un salon**
a dining room	**une salle à manger**
a living room	**une salle de séjour**
a garage	**un garage**
a garden	**un jardin**
to buy a house	**acheter une maison**
a residential area	**un quartier résidentiel**

Understanding the text

aller (v[25])	to go
allô	hello
l'**argent** (nm)	money
aussi (adv)	too
avec (prep)	with
avoir (v[10])	to have
cassé/cassée (adj)	broken
casser (v[1])	to break
une **cassette vidéo** (nf)	video (cassette)
chaud/chaude (adj)	hot
un **cinéma** (nm)	cinema, movie theater
écouter (v[1])	to listen to
s'embêter (v[1])	to be bored
une **émission** (nf)	programme
un/une **enfant** (nmf)	child
faire (v[5])	to do
fait	→ **faire**
l'**horreur** (nf)	loathing
avoir horreur de	to hate
hyper ⓖ (adv)	very
il n'y a que	there is/are only
il y a	there is/are
jouer (v[1])	to play
là (adv)	there
loin (adv)	far
un **loisir** (nm)	leisure
un **magasin** (nm)	shop
un **grand magasin** (nm)	department store
un **magnétoscope** (nm)	video, VCR
une **mère** (nf)	mother
nul/nulle ⓖ (adj)	pathetic
occupé/occupée (adj)	busy
on (pron)	we
passer (v[1])	to put [sb] on
peut	→ **pouvoir**
peux	→ **pouvoir**
pouvoir (v[7])	to be able to, can
quoi (pron)	what
regarder (v[1])	to watch
rester (v[1])	to stay
rien (adv)	nothing
ta (adj)	your
une **télé** ⓖ (nf)	TV
trop (adv)	too much

Pastimes

activities	**les activités** (nfpl)
music	**la musique**
sport	**le sport**
theatre	**le théâtre**
cards	**les cartes** (nfpl)
chess	**les échecs** (nmpl)
draughts, checkers	**le jeu de dames**
clubs	**trèfle** (nm)
diamonds	**carreau** (nm)
hearts	**cœur** (nm)
spades	**pique** (nm)
a suit	**une couleur**
a CD	**un CD**
a CD-ROM	**un cédérom**
a record	**un disque**
a tape	**une cassette**
to listen to music	**écouter de la musique**
to listen to a CD	**écouter un CD**
to watch TV	**regarder la télé**
to play tennis/badminton	**jouer au tennis/badminton**
to play cards	**jouer aux cartes**
to go to the swimming pool	**aller à la piscine**
to go out with friends	**sortir avec des amis**
to read	**lire**
to surf the Net	**surfer** [1] **le net**
I feel like going for a walk	**j'ai envie d'aller me promener**
to go out with friends	**sortir avec des amis**
good idea!	**bonne idée!**

Key Structures

Suggesting activities can be done in several ways:

on peut regarder la télé	we can watch TV
et si on allait au cinéma?	what about going to the cinema?
je vous la passe	I'll put her on
qu'est-ce qu'on fait?	what shall we do?

SOLITUDES

Understanding the text

aller (v[25])	to go
arriver (v[1])	to arrive
avoir (v[10])	to have
un **beau-père** (nm)	stepfather
bien sûr (adv)	of course
à cause de (prep)	because of
un **code** (nm)	door code
communiquer (v[1])	to communicate
contacter (v[1])	to contact
un **demi-frère** (nm)	stepbrother
deux (num)	two
une **enveloppe** (nf)	envelope
une **époque** (nf)	time
évident/évidente (adj)	obvious
facile (adj)	easy
faire (v[5])	to do
un **fax** (nm)	fax machine
un **fax** (nm)	fax message
une **femme** (nf)	wife
une **heure** (nf)	hour
joindre (v[34])	to join
une **ligne** (nf)	line
même (adv)	even
mettre (v[24])	to put
un **numéro** (nm)	number
numéro d'appel	pager
occupé/occupée (adj)	busy
parler (v[1])	to speak
penser à (v[1])	to think of
poster (v[1])	to post, to mail
quelqu'un (pron)	somebody
quoi (pron)	what
savoir (v[17])	to know
la **solitude** (nf)	solitude
un **téléphone** (nm)	telephone
un **timbre** (nm)	(postage) stamp
un **travail** (nm)	work
trois (num)	three

⬅ Communication

a telephone	un téléphone
a fax message	un fax, une télécopie
a fax machine	un fax, un télécopieur
a fax number	un numéro de fax
an email	un mél
telecommunications	les télécommunications (nfpl)
a phone card	une télécarte
a phone box	une cabine téléphonique
a mobile (phone)	un (téléphone) portable
an intercom	un interphone
a Web site	un site Web
e-commerce	le commerce électronique
the post office	la poste
a postman	un facteur
a courier	un coursier
a letter	une lettre
a parcel	un colis
to receive a letter poste restante	recevoir une lettre poste restante
to have one's mail forwarded	faire suivre son courrier
a P.O. box	une boîte postale
the press	la presse
radio	la radio
media	les médias
television	la télévision
evening news	le journal du soir
a daily paper	un quotidien
a weekly magazine	un hebdomadaire

beau-père means both stepfather and father-in-law

Le code is a 4 or 5 digit combination that gives access to a building equipped with an electronic lock.

⬅ Key Structures

ça fait trois heures que j'attends	I have been waiting for three hours
tu sais ce que je fais?	do you know what I do?
penser à quelque chose/quelqu'un	to think of something/somebody
aller chez quelqu'un	to go to somebody's place
elle est allée chez lui	she went to his place

MOTS ET MODE

Understanding the text

alors (adv)	then
un **an** (nm)	year
bleu/bleue (adj)	blue
comment (adv)	how
comprendre (v[8])	to understand
un **concert** (nm)	concert
un **contexte** (nm)	context
continuer (v[1])	to continue
un **coup de pied** (nm)	kick
d'accord	all right
déjà (adv)	already
dépendre (v[6])	to depend
dire (v[14])	to say
environ (adv)	about
épatant/épatante (adj)	spiffing
essayer (v[32])	to try
une **fesse** (nf)	buttock
génial/géniale (adj)	brilliant
giga ⓖ (adj)	neat
un **gigot** (nm)	leg of lamb
inscrire dans (v[35])	to fit into
s'inscrire dans (v[35])	to fit into
une **interaction** (nf)	interaction
lequel/laquelle (pron)	which one
une **maman** (nf)	mum, mom
même (adv)	even
un **menu** (nm)	menu
mille (num)	a thousand
une **mode** (nf)	fashion
un **mot** (nm)	word
ne ... plus (adv)	no longer
ne ... que (adv)	only
un **plan** (nm)	plan
quoi (pron)	what
sais	→ savoir
savoir (v[17])	to know
s'il te plaît	please
une **solution** (nf)	solution
tout (pron)	anything
se vexer (v[1])	to get upset
voir (v[23])	to see

→ Key Structures

génial ne se dit plus	people don't say brilliant any more
génial ne se dit pas	people don't say brilliant
tout se dit	people can say anything
il y a mille ans qu'on ne dit plus génial	people stopped saying brilliant a thousand years ago
il y a 5 ans qu'elle est partie	she left 5 years ago
continue à dire génial	carry on saying brilliant
un coup de pied aux fesses	a kick up your backside

→ Approval and Disapproval

all right	d'accord
great!	super!
approval	l'approbation (nf)
to give one's approval to something	donner son approbation à quelque chose
to agree with somebody about something	être d'accord avec quelqu'un sur quelque chose
I think that was a very good idea	je pense que c'était une très bonne idée
we're very pleased with the result	nous sommes très contents du résultat
it's not bad at all	ce n'est pas mal du tout
how beautiful!	comme c'est beau!
well done!	très bien!
very bad!	très mauvais!
I agree with you on this	je suis d'accord avec toi
I disagree with you on this	je ne suis pas d'accord avec toi
Pierre has agreed to pay	Pierre est d'accord pour payer
to come to an agreement	se mettre or tomber d'accord
we agreed with him that he should leave	nous étions d'accord avec lui sur le fait qu'il devait partir
I couldn't agree more!	je suis entièrement d'accord!
to refuse somebody something	refuser quelque chose à quelqu'un
he refused to pay	il a refusé de payer
with pleasure	avec plaisir
never in all my life!	jamais de la vie!
no way!	pas question!

COMPLAINTE

Ah, c'est toi ma chérie... miracle... on se souvient que j'existe

la dernière fois que j'ai vu ta mère, c'était le 28 octobre à l'enterrement de ton grand-oncle

la dernière fois que j'ai vu ton père, c'était le 9 novembre quand il m'a invitée à déjeuner pour mon anniversaire

alors que je voulais qu'il m'emmène au cinéma.. passons... comment vas-tu?

je

la dernière fois que j'ai vu ton frère Brandon c'était le... non, ton frère c'est Biron, je confonds toujours avec le fils de Jacques

Brandon, je l'ai vu le 1er novembre! Biron, je l'ai vu le 4 novembre à 15 heures...

le jour où je l'ai emmené au parc. Je l'ai ramené à 16 heures 30 et depuis, plus rien.

c'est comme Juliette... elle est venue le 7 à 17 heures et à 17 heures 30, pftt, elle était partie

Nanou insiste pour me voir mais la dernière fois c'était le 25 octobre et elle m'a ennuyée avec ses problèmes!

qu'est-ce que je disais? oui, et toi, depuis le 8 novembre à 18 heures, plus rien... à part un petit coup de fil

d'ailleurs, tu ne viens jamais me voir!

BRETECHER

Understanding the text

aller (v[25])	to be
alors que (conj)	while
un **anniversaire** (nm)	birthday
c'est comme	it's the same with
un/une **chéri/chérie** (nm/f)	darling
un **cinéma** (nm)	cinema, movie theater
comment (adv)	how
une **complainte** (nf)	lament
confondre (v[33])	to mix up, to mistake for
un **coup de fil** ⓖ (nm)	phone call
d'ailleurs (adv)	besides
depuis (prep)	since
dernier/dernière (adj)	last
dire (v[14])	to say
emmener (v[36])	to take
ennuyer (v[20])	to bore
un **enterrement** (nm)	funeral
exister (v[1])	to exist
un **fils** (nm)	son
une **fois** (nf)	time
un **frère** (nm)	brother
un **grand-oncle** (nm)	great uncle
une **heure** (nf)	hour
insister (v[1])	to insist
inviter (v[1])	to invite
jamais (adv)	never
me (pron)	me
une **mère** (nf)	mother
un **miracle** (nm)	miracle
novembre (nm)	november
octobre (nm)	october
un **parc** (nm)	park
partir (v[30])	to leave
un **père** (nm)	father
petit/petite (adj)	short
plus rien	nothing else
pour (prep)	for
un **problème** (nm)	problem
qu'est-ce que	what
ramener (v[36])	to drive back
se souvenir que (v[18])	to remember that
toi (pron)	you
toujours (adv)	always
venir (v[18])	to come
voir (v[23])	to see
vouloir (v[19])	to want

Dates

on Monday	**lundi**
on Tuesdays	**le mardi**
last Wednesday	**mercredi dernier**
last Thursday evening	**jeudi dernier dans la soirée**
next Friday	**vendredi prochain**
Saturday morning	**samedi matin**
on Saturday mornings	**le samedi matin**
in January	**en janvier**
next February	**en février prochain**
last March	**l'année dernière en mars**
in early April	**début avril**
in late May	**fin mai**
in 2000	**en l'an 2000**
since the 1st of May	**depuis le 1er mai**
she came to see me on the 22 June	**elle est venue me voir le 22 juin**
the last time was the 13 November	**la dernière fois, c'était le 13 novembre**

Days of the week and months

Monday	**lundi** (m)
Tuesday	**mardi** (m)
Wednesday	**mercredi** (m)
Thursday	**jeudi** (m)
Friday	**vendredi** (m)
Saturday	**samedi** (m)
Sunday	**dimanche** (m)
January	**janvier** (m)
February	**février** (m)
March	**mars** (m)
April	**avril** (m)
May	**mai** (m)
June	**juin** (m)
July	**juillet** (m)
August	**août** (m)
September	**septembre** (m)
October	**octobre** (m)
November	**novembre** (m)
December	**décembre** (m)

Key Structures

passons!	let's hear no more about it!
je me souviens de ta dernière visite	I remember your last visit
tu te souviens que tu me dois 10 francs?	do you remember that you owe me 10 francs?
la dernière fois que	last time
la dernière fois que je l'ai vue	last time I saw her
inviter quelqu'un à déjeuner	to invite somebody for lunch
comment vas-tu?	how are you?
je confonds toujours ton frère avec ton cousin	I always mistake your brother for your cousin
je voulais qu'il m'emmène au cinéma	I wanted him to take me to the cinema

CHALLENGE

Understanding the text

à plus tard	speak to you later
à plute ⓖ	→ Key Structures
aller (v[25])	to go
alors (adv)	so
américain/américaine (adj)	American
un an (nm)	year
auprès duquel	by comparison with whom
beau/belle (adj)	beautiful
belle	→ beau
belle jeune fille	beautiful young lady
bon (adv)	right
ça (pron)	that
un caneton (nm)	duckling
un challenge (nm)	challenge
un continent (nm)	continent
une cure (nf)	course of treatment
une cure de musées	lots of museum visits
une décision (nf)	decision
depuis (prep)	since
un détour (nm)	detour
dire (v[14])	to say
écouter (v[1])	to listen to
une exploration (nf)	exploration
une fille (nf)	girl
un fils (nm)	son
fréquentable (adj)	respectable
inviter (v[1])	to invite
jeune (adj)	young
un jour (nm)	day
juillet (nm)	July
là (adv)	now
laid/laide (adj)	ugly
long/longue (adj)	long
m' = me (pron)	me

maintenant (adv)	now
un musée (nm)	museum
la nature (nf)	nature
naturellement (adv)	naturally
nous (pron)	us
obligatoire (adj)	compulsory
être (v[3]) obligé/obligée	to have to
un père (nm)	father
peux	→ pouvoir
ne ... plus (adv)	no longer
un pote ⓖ (nm)	mate, pal
pouvoir (v[7])	to be able to
prendre (v[8])	to take
pris	→ prendre
qui (pron)	who
un ranch (nm)	ranch
rappeler (v[9])	to phone back
une semaine (nf)	week
te (pron)	you
voilà	there you are
y (pron)	there

J'ai pris the big décision
Mixing English words with French is
supposed to be trendy.

→ Key Structures

à plute is a shortened slang form of à plus tard

à plus tard	speak to you later
	see you later

Another popular expression formed on the same principle

astap is a shortened form of à cet après-midi

à cet après-midi	see you in the afternoon

depuis + present tense

il nous invite depuis 10 ans	he's been inviting us for 10 years

il faut que + subjunctive

il faut que j'écoute	I must listen
il faut que je parte	I must go
il faut que tu ailles au garage	you must go to the garage

un fils de dix-sept ans	a seventeen-year-old son
un voyage de trois semaines	a three-week trip
un livre de 200 pages	a 200-page book

pouvoir + infinitive = to be able + infinitive

je peux pas te parler	I cannot speak to you

je suis obligée d'y aller?	do I have to go?

y, which means there, is not translated.

→ Travelling

a plane	un avion
a train	un train
a car	une voiture
a coach	un autocar
a motorway	une autoroute
the airport	l'aéroport (nm)
the (railway) station	la gare
the coach station	la gare routière
the port	le port
a hotel	un hôtel
an inn	une auberge
a youth hostel	une auberge de jeunesse
a guesthouse	une pension de famille
vacancies	chambres à louer
no vacancies	complet
half board	la demi-pension
a single room	une chambre pour une personne
a double room	une chambre pour deux personnes
an en-suite room	une chambre avec salle d'eau
the reception desk	la réception
full board	la pension complète
breakfast	le petit déjeuner
do you have a double room?	est-ce que vous avez une chambre pour deux?
l'hôtel est complet	the hotel is full
to book a room for 3 nights	réserver une chambre pour 3 nuits

POURBOIRE

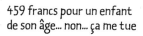

Understanding the text

un **âge** (nm)	age
aller (v[25])	to go
avec (prep)	with
avoir (v[10])	to have
une **bricole** (nf)	little something
un **cadeau** (nm)	present
celui-là (pron)	that one
changer (v[15])	to change
un/une **chéri/chérie** (nm/f)	darling
déjà (adv)	already
dire (v[14])	to say
donner (v[11])	to give
un/une **enfant** (nmf)	child
faire (v[5])	to do
	to make
fasse	→ faire
un **fils** (nm)	son
fou/folle (adj)	mad, crazy
des **gens** (nmpl)	people
gentil/gentille (adj)	kind
giga ⓒ (adj)	neat
la **joie** (nf)	joy
laisser (v[1])	to leave
malade (adj)	ill, sick
rendre (v[6]) **malade**	to make [sb] sick
un **merci** (nm)	thank you
oublier (v[28])	to forget
un **papa** (nm)	dad, pop
pas la peine	not worth it
penser à (v[1])	to think about
peut	→ pouvoir
pour (prep)	for
un **pourboire** (nm)	tip
pourrais	→ pouvoir
pouvoir (v[7])	to be able to, can
un **prix** (nm)	price
quand (conj)	when
qui (pron)	who
radin/radine ⓒ (adj)	stingy
remarquer (v[1])	to notice
suffire (v[37])	to be enough
ça suffit	that's enough
tellement (adv)	so (much)
ton (adj)	your
tout (pron)	everything
trop (adv)	too much
tuer (v[1])	to kill
va	→ aller
veux	→ vouloir
voilà	there you are
vouloir (v[19])	to want

⬔ Money

John earns 10,000 francs a month	**John gagne 10 000 francs par mois**
a well-paid job	**un travail bien payé**
I've been given a pay rise	**j'ai eu une augmentation**
they have money problems	**ils ont des problèmes d'argent**
her uncle is a millionaire	**son oncle est millionnaire**
a bank	**une banque**
a bank account	**un compte en banque**
savings	**les économies** (nfpl)
a savings bank	**une caisse d'épargne**
a building society	**société d'investissement et de crédit immobilier**
a safe	**un coffre-fort**
to make a deposit	**effectuer un dépôt**
to make a withdrawal	**effectuer un retrait**
I must get money at the bank	**il faut que je retire de l'argent à la banque**
an ATM	**un distributeur automatique de billets**
to change money	**changer de l'argent**
small change	**la petite monnaie**
a coin	**une pièce**
a banknote	**un billet de banque**
a cheque book	**un chéquier**
a credit card	**une carte de crédit**
a payment card	**une carte de paiement**
insert your card	**insérer votre carte**
key your PIN	**tapez votre code**
to save money	**faire des économies**
to borrow	**emprunter**
to lend	**prêter**
she owes me money	**elle me doit de l'argent**
a £100 cheque	**un chèque de 100£**

⬔ Key Structures

aller + infinitive is used to express the future tense

il va être furieux	he's going to be furious
je vais leur dire	I'll tell them

faire des cadeaux	to give presents

vouloir que + subjunctive

que veux-tu que je fasse?	what do you want me to do?

L'AMITIÉ

je ne comprends pas ce que tu trouves à cette andouille de Trevor

il est giga

tu n'y connais rien... moi j'ai un flair pour les mecs

il craint

il faut anticiper un max Trevor est encore jeune, j'admets, mais à 18 ans il sera canon

il a un gros cul

c'est nul! il achète ses jeans à Moscou et il a deux paires de Weston, je m'excuse

tout le monde dit que tu es amoureuse de lui

je n'ai encore rien décidé d'ailleurs je ne te le dirai pas, tu le répèterais à tout le monde

il t'embrasse?

même à toi je n'aime pas tellement parler de ça... je suis très prude comme femme

alors qu'est-ce que tu fais quand tu sors avec lui?

on s'éclate... je ne comprends pas tout ce qu'il m'explique mais toi tu ne comprendrais rien

et quand as-tu l'intention de conclure?

ce que tu peux manquer de tact et de discrétion par moments, ça me tue

pose-moi encore des questions

BRETECHER

Understanding the text

acheter (v[31])	to buy
admettre (v[24])	to admit
aimer (v[1])	to love
alors (adv)	so
l'**amitié** (nf)	friendship
amoureux/amoureuse (adj)	in love
un **an** (nm)	year
une **andouille** ◎ (nf)	fool
anticiper (v[1])	to anticipate
avec (prep)	with
ça (pron)	that
canon ◎ (adj)	gorgeous
ce que	what
comprendre (v[8])	to understand
conclure (v[38])	to conclude
connaître (v[30])	to know
craindre ◎ (v[39])	to be a prat
un **cul** ◎ (nm)	bottom
d'ailleurs	besides
décider (v[1])	to make up one's mind
dire à (v[14])	to tell
la **discrétion** (nf)	discretion
s'éclater ◎ (v[1])	to have a good time
s'excuser (v[1])	to apologize
embrasser (v[1])	to kiss
encore (adv)	again
expliquer (v[1])	to explain
faire (v[5])	to do
une **femme** (nf)	woman
le **flair** (nm)	flair
giga ◎ (adj)	neat
gros/grosse (adj)	big
imaginer (v[1])	to imagine
une **intention** (nf)	intention
un **jean** (nm)	jeans
jeune (adj)	young
lui (pron)	him
m' (pron)	me
mais (conj)	but
manquer de (v[1])	to be lacking in
un **mec** ◎ (nm)	guy
même (adj)	even
Moscou (nprm)	Moscow
nul/nulle ◎ (adj)	pathetic
on (pron)	we
une **paire** (nf)	pair
par moments	at times
parler (v[1])	to talk
poser (v[1]) **des questions**	to ask questions
prude (adj)	prudish
qu'est-ce que	what
quand (conj)	when
répéter (v[26])	to repeat
rien (adv)	nothing
sortir avec (v[4])	to go out with
t' = te (pron)	you
le **tact** (nm)	tact
tellement (adv)	so much
toi (pron)	you
tout (adj)	every
tout le monde	everybody
trouver (v[1])	to find
tuer (v[1])	to kill
un **max** ◎	a lot
Weston	Weston shoes

⬔ ## Love and Relationships

a friend	un/une ami/amie
a boyfriend/girlfriend	un/une petit ami/petite amie
an acquaintance	une relation
an acquaintance	une connaissance
a friend	un/une copain/copine
to go out with	sortir avec
to chat up	draguer
to meet	se rencontrer
we met in Grenoble	nous nous sommes rencontrés à Grenoble
do you come here often?	vous venez souvent ici?
to love somebody	aimer quelqu'un
to shake hands with somebody	serrer la main de quelqu'un
to kiss somebody	embrasser quelqu'un
to be fond of	bien aimer quelqu'un
to get on with somebody	bien s'entendre avec quelqu'un
to hate somebody	détester quelqu'un
I miss you	tu me manques

⬔ ## Key Structures

cette andouille de Trevor	this fool Trevor
il craint	he's a prat
ça craint	it's the pits
tu n'y connais rien	you don't know the first thing about it
ce que tu peux manquer de tact!	you can be so tactless!
ce que tu es bête!	you can be so stupid!

INVASION

Understanding the text

¹/₄ (un quart) (nm)	a quarter
aborder (v[1])	to tackle
un/une **Africain/Africaine** (nm/f)	African
un **antibiotique** (nm)	antibiotic
appeler (v[9])	to phone
avec (prep)	with
une **balance** (nf) **des paiements**	balance of payments
bîbîp	beep
bon! (adv)	right!
bouillir (v[40])	to boil
une **casserole** (nf)	saucepan
une **classe** (nf)	class, classroom
compliqué/compliquée (adj)	complicated
déranger (v[15])	to disturb
dire à (v[14])	to tell
l' **eau** (nf)	water
écouter (v[1])	to listen
envoyer (v[2])	to send
épluché/épluchée (adj)	peeled
être (v[31]) **hospitalisé/hospitalisée**	to be taken to hospital
se faire (v[5]) **voler quelque chose**	to have something stolen
la **France** (nf)	France
une **grand-mère** (nf)	grandmother
une **heure** (nf)	hour
une **invasion** (nf)	invasion
jamais (adv)	never
laisser (v[1])	to let
lui (pron)	him/her
malade (adj)	ill, sick
une **mère** (nf)	mother
mettre (v[24])	to put
parrainer (v[1])	to sponsor
une **patate** ⊚ (nf)	spud
un **pense-bête** (nm)	reminder
un **père** (nm)	father
petit/petite (adj)	young
un **portable** (nm)	mobile
premier/première (adj)	first
proposer (v[1])	to offer
un **rendez-vous** (nm)	appointment
répéter (v[26])	to repeat
retrouver (v[1])	to find (something that was lost)
le **sel** (nm)	salt
une **sœur** (nf)	sister
un **téléphone portable** (nm)	mobile phone
voir (v[23])	to see
une **voiture** (nf)	car
voler (v[1])	to steal

⊡ On the phone

to pick up the phone	**décrocher**
to hang up	**raccrocher**
the receiver	**le combiné**
a mobile phone	**un (téléphone) portable**
a cordless telephone	**un téléphone sans fil**
to dial the number	**composer le numéro**
the dialling tone	**la tonalité**
an answering machine	**un répondeur automatique**
a voice mail	**une messagerie vocale**
a telephone directory	**un annuaire**
the yellow pages	**les pages jaunes**
the telephone directory	**les pages blanches**
to be ex-directory	**être sur liste rouge**
extension number	**numéro de poste**
extension 5148, please	**poste 5148, s'il vous plaît**
I'll put you through	**je vous passe votre correspondant**
it's engaged	**c'est occupé**
it's ringing	**ça sonne**
there's no answer	**ça ne répond pas**
hello!	**allô, bonjour!**
hold the line	**ne quittez pas**
speaking!	**à l'appareil!**
one moment, please	**un instant, je vous prie**
I'll call back later	**je rappellerai plus tard**
who is calling please?	**c'est de la part de qui?**
it's a personal call	**c'est personnel**
Mrs Leroy is on the phone	**Madame Leroy est en ligne**
a phonecard	**une télécarte**
you've got the wrong number	**c'est une erreur**
who do you want to talk to?	**qui demandez-vous?**
you have reached Grace's answering machine	**vous êtes bien sur le répondeur de Grace**
please leave your message after the tone	**merci de laisser un message après le signal sonore**

> In French, telephone numbers are given using double figures, e.g. for **0186555676** you say 'zéro-un quatre-vingt-six cinquante cinq cinquante-six soixante-seize'

⊡ Key Structures

the verb **aller** + infinitive is used to express immediate future

nous allons aborder	we are going to tackle
il va te téléphoner	he's going to ring you

the verb **venir** + **de** + infinitive is used to express immediate past

il vient de me retrouver	he's just found me
je viens de le voir	I've just seen him

the verb **se faire** + infinitive is used to express an action performed (directly or indirectly on the subject)

se faire voler son portable	to have one's mobile stolen
je me suis fait couper les cheveux	I've had my hair cut
il s'est fait agresser	he was mugged

AU BERCAIL

Understanding the text

aller (v[25])	to go
alors (adv)	then
américain/américaine (adj)	American
au bercail ◎	at home
bien (adv)	perfectly
c'est le moment	you chose your moment
la **Californie** (nprf)	California
ce soir	tonight
chez (prep)	to
compter (v[1])	to intend
un/une **cousin/cousine** (nm/f)	cousin
dégoûter (v[1])	to make [sb] sick
un **dimanche** (nm)	Sunday
drôle (adj)	funny
s'éclater ◎ (v[1])	to have a great time
un/une **enfant** (nmf)	child
enfin bon (adv)	anyway
envoyer (v[2])	to send
faire (v[5])	to do
une **famille** (nf)	family
giga ◎ (adj)	neat
les **grandes vacances** (nfpl)	summer holiday, summer vacation
ici	here
un/une **invité/invitée** (nm/f)	guest
moi (pron)	me
motiver (v[1])	to motivate
Pâques	Easter
des **parents** (nmpl)	parents
peut-être (adv)	maybe
un **projet** (nm)	plan
pas question d'aller	no way will I go
quand (adv)	when
qu'est-ce que...	what...
quoi (pron)	what
savoir (v[17])	to know
tout à fait (adv)	completely
des **vacances** (ntpl)	holiday, vacation

 Time off

seaside holiday/vacation	**vacances** (nfpl) **à la mer**
skiing holiday/vacation	**vacances de neige**
Christmas holiday/vacation	**vacances de Noël**
Easter holiday/vacation	**vacances de Pâques**
Summer holiday/vacation	**grandes vacances**
half-term	**petites vacances**
to go on holiday/vacation	**partir en vacances**
where are you going for your holidays/vacation?	**où allez-vous en vacances?**
I had a lovely holiday/vacation in Greece	**j'ai passé de merveilleuses vacances en Grèce**
did you take a holiday/vacation this winter?	**vous avez pris des vacances cet hiver?**
yes, we went skiing with the children	**oui, nous sommes allés faire du ski avec les enfants**
to go on a camping holiday/vacation	**partir en camping**
to take ten days' holiday/vacation	**prendre dix jours de congé**
four weeks' holiday/vacation with pay	**quatre semaines de congés payés**

 Key Structures

il y a can be followed by a singular or a plural

il y a un invité	there is a guest
il y a des invités	there are guests

on can be used to talk of a group you are part of

qu'est-ce qu'on fait dimanche?	what are we doing on Sunday?
qu'est-ce qu'on fait pour les vacances de Pâques?	what are we doing at Easter?
qu'est-ce qu'on fait aux grandes vacances?	what are we doing during the summer holiday?
quand est-ce qu'on va en Californie?	when are we going to California?

il paraît que is used to express a rumour

il paraît qu'il y a des parents qui motivent leurs enfants avec des giga projets	apparently there are parents who motivate their children with super plans

- **Les Puces** is a famous fleamarket in Paris.
- **Noirmoutier** is an island in the Atlantic ocean; it is renowned as a sea resort.

LE CERVEAU

Trevor on va être en retard

je ne viens pas, je suis sur un coup

tu exagères

une demi-heure de bus, tu me téléphones même pas... tu es impossible

ça m'a pris subitement, tu peux pas comprendre

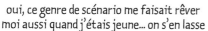

ouopopoh yeah

Un copain à moi a réussi à percer le code de la BNP de la rue Victor Macé

oui, ce genre de scénario me faisait rêver moi aussi quand j'étais jeune... on s'en lasse

il y a plus intéressant... l'argent n'est pas tout dans la vie

arrête!

tu pourrais faire passer six zéros sur ton compte tu ne le ferais pas?

non

moi je suis sur le réseau SPAN de NASA alors les esclaves toujours en train de courir après un milliard moi ça me plie

je peux téléphoner?

dans l'entrée

deux francs

Understanding the text

l'**argent** (nm)	money
arrêter (v[1])	to stop
aussi (adv)	also
un **bus** (nm)	bus
un **cerveau** (nm)	brain
un **code** (nm)	code
comprendre (v[8])	to understand
un **compte** (nm)	account
un /une **copain/copine** (nm/f)	friend
un **coup** (nm)	job, trick
être (v[3]) **sur un coup** ⊚	to be onto something big
courir aprés (v[49])	to run after
demi-heure (nf)	half an hour
deux	two
en train de	in the process of
une **entrée** (nf)	entrance
un/une **esclave** (nm/f)	slave
être (v[3])	to be
exagérer (v[26])	to exaggerate
faire (v[5])	to make
un **franc** (nm)	franc
un **genre** (nm)	sort
il y a	there is, there are
impossible (adj)	impossible
intéressant/intéressante (adj)	interesting
jeune (adj)	young
se lasser de (v[1])	to grow tired of
même (adv)	even
moi (pron)	me
passer (v[1])	to transfer
percer (v[12])	to crack
peux	→ **pouvoir**
plier ⊚ (v[28])	to make [sb] laugh
plus (adv)	more
pourrais	→ **pouvoir**
pouvoir (v[7])	to be able to, can
prendre (v[8])	to take
ça m'a pris/prise	it took me
quand (conj)	when
un **réseau** (nm)	network
un **retard** (nm)	delay
être (v[3]) **en retard**	to be late
réussir (v[41])	to succeed
rêver (v[1])	to dream
un **scénario** (nm)	scenario
six	six
subitement (adv)	suddenly
téléphoner (v[1])	to make a phone call
toujours (adv)	always
tout (pron)	everything
venir (v[18])	to come
une **vie** (nf)	life
un **zéro** (nm)	nought, zero

➡ Computing and the Internet

a computer	**un ordinateur**
a screen	**un écran**
a keyboard	**un clavier**
a mouse	**une souris**
a mousepad	**un tapis de souris**
email	**le courrier électronique**
to send an email	**envoyer un mél**
to receive an email	**recevoir un mél**
an email address	**une adresse électronique**
to click	**cliquer**
to save	**enregistrer**
to back up	**faire une copie de sauvegarde**
to send	**envoyer**
check mail	**vérifier courrier**
an attachment	**une pièce jointe**
delete	**supprimer**
the inbox	**la boîte d'arrivée**
the outbox	**la boîte d'envoi**
an address book	**un carnet d'adresses**
a new message	**un nouveau message**
reply	**répondre**
reply all	**répondre à tous les destinataires**
forward	**faire suivre**
attach	**joindre un fichier**
a filter	**un filtre**
print	**imprimer**
a folder	**un dossier**
a directory	**un répertoire**
a file	**un fichier**

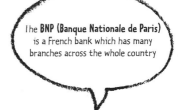

The **BNP (Banque Nationale de Paris)** is a French bank which has many branches across the whole country

➡ Key Structures

être en retard	to be late
le train était en retard	the train was late
je suis en retard dans mon travail	I'm late with my work

SOUCIS

Understanding the text

agresser (v[1])	to mug
se faire (v[5]) **agresser**	to be mugged
appeler (v[9])	to phone
avec (prep)	with
bien (adv)	right
chez (prep)	at
être (v[3]) **censé/censée**	to be supposed to
content/contente (adj)	satisfied
devoir (v[42])	to have to, must
dire à (v[14])	to tell
dormir (v[41])	to sleep
encore (adv)	still
espionner (v[1])	to spy on
essayer (v[32])	to try
faire (v[5])	to do
un garçon (nm)	boy
une heure (nf)	hour
jamais (adv)	never
là (adv)	there
mais (conj)	but
un matin (nm)	morning
une nuit (nf)	night
où (adv)	where
parce que (conj)	because
passer (v[1])	to spend
peux	→ **pouvoir**
un pied (nm)	foot
à pied	on foot
un point (nm)	full stop, period
pour ne pas	so as not
pourquoi (adv)	why
pouvoir (v[7])	to be able to, can
prochain/prochaine (adj)	next
être (v[3]) **privé/privée de sorties**	to be grounded
puisque (conj)	since
qu'est-ce que	what
qui (pron)	who
rentrer (v[1])	to come home
réveiller (v[1])	to wake up
une rue (nf)	street
savoir (v[17])	to know
sortie (nf)	outing
un souci (nm)	worry
se faire (v[5]) **du souci pour**	to worry about
le stop (nm)	hitching
faire (v[5]) **du stop**	to hitch
un taxi (nm)	taxi
téléphoner (v[1])	to phone
tout (pron)	everything
tout le monde	everybody
vouloir (v[19])	to want

⮕ Emotions

happiness	**le bonheur**
sadness	**la tristesse**
worry	**le souci**
fear	**la peur**
anger	**la colère**
love	**l'amour** (nm)
jealousy	**la jalousie**
pleasure	**le plaisir**
to laugh	**rire**
to smile	**sourire**
to cry	**pleurer**
to shout	**crier**

to be pleased about something	**être content/contente de quelque chose**
I'm so happy for you	**je suis si heureux/heureuse pour toi**
I laugh because I'm happy	**je ris parce que je suis heureux/heureuse**
to be in love	**être amoureux/amoureuse**
they love each other	**ils s'aiment**
she fancies him	**il lui plaît**
he's jealous	**il est jaloux**
to be afraid of something	**avoir peur de quelque chose**
we were so scared	**nous étions terrifiés**
to worry about somebody/something	**se faire du souci pour quelqu'un/quelque chose**
don't worry	**ne t'inquiète pas**
to be angry at somebody	**être en colère contre quelqu'un**
he was furious	**il était furieux**
she regrets what she did	**elle regrette ce qu'elle a fait**
I'm sorry	**je suis désolé/désolée**

⮕ Key Structures

d'où sors-tu?	where have you been?
d'où venez-vous?	where do you come from?
d'où es-tu?	where are you from?
chez Bergère	at Bergère's place
on a dormi chez Mathilde	we slept at Mathilde's house/flat
où tu es la nuit	where you are at night
il travaille la nuit	he works at night

LE BOULET

c'est ma copine Coco qui demande si tu veux baby-sitter ce soir

BABY-SITTER CE SOIR

oui bonjour

oui

vous payez combien?

oui... c'est tout? je préfère plus... et les deux taxis...

ok oui

vous avez un grand écran... quelle marque? oui giga!

une antenne parabolique? vous recevez combien de chaînes? GIGA

et si tout est nul sur les 45 chaînes vous avez quoi comme vidéos? oui.. giga! et je peux me servir d'internet?

oh n'importe quoi: du saucisson, des chips, des cornichons... vous avez des glaces? oui des bonbons n'importe quel parfum, sauf fruit de la passion

biberon?

eh j'avais oublié j'ai un contrôle de maths demain matin

alors ça marche?

ALORS ÇA MARCHE?

non, c'est galère... il y a un môme

BRETECHER

Understanding the text

une **antenne** (nf)	aerial
une **antenne parabolique** (nf)	satellite dish
baby-sitter (v[1])	to babysit
un **biberon** (nm)	baby bottle, nursing bottle
un **bonbon** (nm)	sweet
une **chaîne** (nf)	channel
des **chips** (nfpl)	crisps, potato chips
combien (adv)	how much
un **contrôle** (nm)	test
une **copine** (nf)	friend
demander (v[1])	to ask
un **écran** (nm)	screen
un **fruit de la passion** (nm)	passion fruit
une **galère** ⓖ (nf)	hell
giga ⓖ (adj)	neat
une **glace** (nf)	ice cream
grand/grande (adj)	large
n'importe quoi	anything
marcher (v[1])	to work
une **marque** (nf)	make
les **maths** (nfpl)	maths
un/une **môme** ⓖ (nmf)	brat
nul/nulle ⓖ (adj)	pathetic
oublier (v[28])	to forget
un **parfum** (nm)	flavour
payer (v[32])	to pay
plus (adv)	more
préférer (v[26])	to prefer
recevoir (v[43])	to get
un **saucisson** (nm)	pork sausage
se servir de (v[4])	to use
un **soir** (nm)	evening
ce soir	tonight
un **taxi** (nm)	taxi
les deux taxis	taxi both ways
tout (pron)	everything
c'est tout	that's all
une **vidéo** (nf)	video
vouloir (v[19])	to want

Food and Drink

a banana	une **banane**
a cherry	une **cerise**
a nectarine	une **nectarine**
a peach	une **pêche**
a pear	une **poire**
a plum	une **prune**
a raspberry	une **framboise**
a strawberry	une **fraise**
an apricot	un **abricot**
an orange	une **orange**
grape	du **raisin**
a Brussel sprout	un **chou de Bruxelles**
a cabbage	un **chou**
a carrot	une **carotte**
a cucumber	un **concombre**
a green bean	un **haricot vert**
a lettuce	une **salade**
a pea	un **petit pois**
a pepper	un **poivron**
a potato	une **pomme de terre**
an onion	un **oignon**
garlic	l'**ail** (nm)
beef	le **bœuf**
chicken	le **poulet**
fish	le **poisson**
lamb	l'**agneau** (nm)
pork	le **porc**
poultry	la **volaille**
veal	le **veau**
a coffee with milk	un **crème**
beer	la **bière**
cider	le **cidre**
coffee	le **café**
fruit juice	le **jus de fruit**
lemonade	la **limonade**
wine	le **vin**
white wine	le **vin blanc**
red wine	le **vin rouge**
water	l'**eau** (nf)
mineral water	l'**eau minérale**
sparkling water	l'**eau gazeuse**
still water	l'**eau plate**
tea	le **thé**

Key Structures

demander si	to ask if
ma copine demande si tu veux baby-sitter	my friend asks if you want to babysit
il m'a demandé si je voulais aller au cinéma avec lui	he asked me if I wanted to go to the pictures with him
vouloir + infinitive	
tu veux babysitter	you want to babysit
je ne veux pas aller au cinéma	I do not want to go to the pictures
vous avez quoi comme chaînes?	what channels do you have?

ANNIVERSAIRE

je vais faire quelque chose pour l'anniversaire de ta mère

peut-être un grand dessin de notre arbre généalogique

ou une BD couleur sur sa vie avec son mari

ou alors je pourrais lui enregistrer une cassette avec des chansons de son époque

et entre les chansons, je dirais des choses gentilles

ou alors je pourrais écrire une pièce où elle serait la star... on jouerait dedans aussi

je pourrais la filmer avec la caméra vidéo de Trevor

ça lui ferait plaisir, non?

encore plus que tu ne crois

le demi-frère de Bergère a tout le matériel, je fais le montage

ça va prendre un temps fou

tout peut être bouclé en une semaine à condition de sauter les repas

oui mais son anniversaire est demain... si tu lui envoyais simplement une petite carte

une petite carte?

ah non... là c'est trop fatigant!

BRETECHER

Understanding the text

aller (v[25])	→ Key Structures
alors (adv)	then
un **anniversaire** (nm)	birthday
un **arbre** (nm)	tree
un **arbre généalogique** (nm)	family tree
aussi (adv)	too
une **BD** (nf)	cartoon strip
boucler (v[1])	to finish
une **caméra** (nf)	camera
une **caméra vidéo** (nf)	camcorder
une **carte** (nf)	card
une **cassette** (nf)	cassette
une **chanson** (nf)	song
une **chose** (nf)	thing
une **condition** (nf)	condition
une **couleur** (nf)	colour
croire (v[44])	to believe
dedans (adv)	inside
demain (adv)	tomorrow
un **demi-frère** (nm)	stepbrother
un **dessin** (nm)	drawing
écrire (v[35])	to write
encore plus	even more
enregistrer (v[1])	to record
envoyer (v[2])	to send
une **époque** (nf)	time
faire (v[5])	to do
fatigant/fatigante	tiring
filmer (v[1])	to film
fou/folle (adj)	mad, crazy
gentil/gentille (adj)	kind
grand/grande (adj)	large
jouer (v[1])	to perform
là (adv)	now
mais (conj)	but
un **mari** (nm)	husband
un **matériel** (nm)	equipment
une **mère** (nf)	mother
un **montage** (nm)	editing
petit/petite (adj)	little
peut-être (adv)	maybe
une **pièce** (nf)	play
un **plaisir** (nm)	pleasure
pouvoir (v[7])	to be able to
prendre (v[8])	to take
quelque chose	something
un **repas** (nm)	meal
sauter (v[1])	to jump
une **semaine** (nf)	week
si (conj)	if
simplement (adv)	simply
une **star** (nf)	star
un **temps** (nm)	time
une **vie** (nf)	life

⇨ Art and Literature

painting	**la peinture**
sculpture	**la sculpture**
engraving	**la gravure**
drawing	**le dessin**
music	**la musique**
theatre	**le théâtre**
cinema	**le cinéma**
dancing	**la danse**
literature	**la littérature**
architecture	**l'architecture** (nf)
an art gallery	**une galerie d'art**
a museum	**un musée**
a concert hall	**une salle de concert**
a theatre	**un théâtre**
poetry	**la poésie**
a painter	**un peintre**
a sculptor	**un sculpteur**
a work of art	**une œuvre d'art**
an exhibition	**une exposition**

⇨ Key Structures

BD couleur	cartoon strip in colour
TV couleur	colour TV
faire plaisir à quelqu'un	to make somebody happy
ça va prendre un temps fou	it will take ages
si tu lui envoyais une carte	what about sending her a card
à condition de + infinitive	provided
à condition que + subjunctive	provided

aller + infinitive is used to express the future tense

je vais faire quelque chose	I'm going to do something
il va être furieux	he's going to be furious
je vais leur dire	I'll tell them

BAVURE

Understanding the text

alors que (conj)	even though
amazonien/amazonienne (adj)	Amazonian
l'**Asie centrale** (nprf)	Central Asia
une **bavure** (nf)	blunder
choisir (v[41])	to choose
une **copie** (nf)	paper
une **évolution** (nf)	evolution
une **forêt** (nf)	forest
injuste (adj)	unfair
mais (conj)	but
mettre (v[24])	to put
moi (pron)	me
naturel/naturelle (adj)	natural
passer (v[11])	to pass
pomper ⊚ (v[11])	to crib, to copy
premier/première (adj)	first
une **ressource** (nf)	resource
second/seconde (adj)	second
un **sujet** (nm)	subject
tout (pron)	everything
vous (pron)	you

⊡ Key Structures

Vous avez mis 15 à Mathieu Fourny	You gave Mathieu Fourny 15
c'est injuste	it's unfair
premier/première is often abbreviated as **1er/1ère**.	
au 1er étage	on the first floor

The abbreviation is also used for dates: **le 1er janvier** 1st January

According to the most current marking system in France the highest mark is **20** and the lowest **0**. Anything below **10** is a fail.

⊡ The Earth

the earth	**la terre**
the sky	**le ciel**
the stars	**les étoiles**
the sun	**le soleil**
the moon	**la lune**
the rainforest	**la forêt tropicale**
the ocean	**l'océan** (nm)
a continent	**un continent**
a mountain	**une montagne**
a river	**une rivière**
the northern/southern hemisphere	**l'hémisphère** (nm) **nord/sud**
the Arctic/Antarctic circle	**le cercle polaire arctique/antarctique**
the North/South Pole	**le pôle Nord/Sud**
the equator	**l'équateur** (nm)
at the seaside	**à la mer**
a seaside resort	**une station balnéaire**
the tide is coming in	**la marée monte**
the tide is going out	**la marée descend**
in the mountains	**en montagne**
snow	**la neige**
a torrent	**un torrent**
a ski resort	**une station de ski**
a ski-lift	**un remonte-pente**
the weather	**le temps**
rain	**la pluie**
hail	**la grêle**
thunder	**le tonnerre**
lightning	**un éclair**
frost	**le gel**
black ice	**le verglas**
fog	**le brouillard**
what's the weather like?	**quel temps fait-il?**
it's fine today	**il fait beau aujourd'hui**
it's cold	**il fait froid**
it's raining	**il pleut**
it's raining cats and dogs	**il pleut des cordes**
it's snowing	**il neige**
the forecast is snow	**la météo annonce de la neige**

KARMA

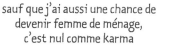

Understanding the text

un **acte** (nm)	action
antérieur/antérieure (adj)	previous
aussi (adv)	also
avaler (v[1])	to swallow
avoir (v[10])	to have
un **calmant** (nm)	sedative
une **chambre** (nf)	bedroom
une **chance** (nf)	chance
contre (prep)	against
un **destin** (nm)	fate
déterminé/déterminée (adj)	determined
devenir (v[18])	to become
dire (v[14])	to say
donc (conj)	therefore
dur/dure (adj)	hard
énerver (v[1])	to get on [sb's] nerves
un **exemple** (nm)	example
faire (v[5])	to do
une **femme de ménage** (nf)	cleaner
futur/future (adj)	future
habiter (v[1])	to live
un **jour** (nm)	day
un **karma** (nm)	karma
maudire (v[45])	to curse
mettre (v[24])	to put
le **mieux**	the best
moi (pron)	me
le **moins possible**	as little as possible
nul/nulle ⑤ (adj)	pathetic
un **palais** (nm)	palace
une **pile** (nf)	battery

un **point** (nm)	full stop, period
pouvoir (v[7])	to be able to
quoi (pron)	what
ranger (v[15])	to tidy up
se **retourner** (v[1])	to turn around
sauf que (conj)	except that
somptueux/somptueuse (adj)	sumptuous
de **temps en temps**	from time to time
tout (pron)	everything
un **point c'est tout**	that's final
une **vie** (nf)	life
vouloir (v[19])	to want

⊡ Key Structures

ça veut dire quoi "karma"?	what does 'karma' mean?
ça veut dire destin	it means fate
ça veut dire qu'il faut partir	it means it's time to leave
le mieux est de ne rien faire	it's best to do nothing
le mieux possible	as well as possible
le moins possible	as little as possible

⊡ Health

an illness, a disease	**une maladie**
to be in good shape	**être en forme**
to be ill	**être malade**
I have a headache	**j'ai mal à la tête**
where does it hurt?	**où est-ce que vous avez mal?**
my elbow hurts	**j'ai mal au coude**
did you hurt yourself?	**tu t'es fait mal?**
she broke her arm	**elle s'est cassé le bras**
I twisted my ankle	**je me suis tordu la cheville**
I sprained my ankle	**je me suis foulé la cheville**
to be operated on	**se faire opérer**
flu	**la grippe**
a cold	**un rhume**
food poisoning	**un empoisonnement alimentaire**
a mosquito bite	**une piqûre de moustique**
a spot	**un bouton**
to be sea sick	**avoir le mal de mer**
hayfever	**le rhume des foins**
asthma	**l'asthme** (nm)
to suffer from asthma	**avoir de l'asthme**
to sneeze	**éternuer**
to cough	**tousser**
to be tired	**être fatigué**
my ankle is swollen	**ma cheville est enflée**
a scar	**une cicatrice**
to be allergic to penicillin	**être allergique à la pénicilline**

PHOTO

je suis horrible, ce n'est pas moi du tout

moi aussi je suis horrible, ce n'est pas moi du tout

tu crois que c'est vraiment nous?

en tous cas je reconnais ton blouson

ce doit être une fille qui était avant nous et qui avait le même blouson que moi

oui et l'autre avait le même col roulé que moi

je déteste qu'une autre fille soit habillée comme moi

moi aussi... on va refaire des photos avec d'autres fringues

BRETECHER

Understanding the text

aussi (adv)	too
avant (prep)	before
un **blouson** (nm)	jacket
un **col roulé** (nm)	polo neck
comme moi	like me
croire (v[44])	to believe
d'autres fringues	other clothes
détester (v[1])	to hate
du tout	at all
en tous cas	in any case
être (v[3])	to be
une **fille** (nf)	girl
des **fringues** Ⓡ (nfpl)	clothes, gear
habillé/habillée (adj)	dressed
horrible (adj)	horrid
l'autre (pron)	the other
moi (pron)	me
une **photo** (nf)	photo
reconnaître (v[30])	recognize
refaire (v[5])	to do again
suis	→ être
vraiment (adv)	really

Clothes

a garment	**un vêtement**
a belt	**une ceinture**
a shirt	**une chemise**
a blouse	**un chemisier**
a dress	**une robe**
a dressing gown	**une robe de chambre**
tights	**des collants** (nmpl)
gloves	**des gants** (nmpl)
jeans	**un jean**
a swimming costume	**un maillot de bain**
a coat	**un manteau**
a pair of trousers	**un pantalon**
a jacket	**une veste**
underwear	**les sous-vêtements** (nmpl)
a bra	**un soutien-gorge**
a pair of knickers	**une culotte, un slip**
a pair of underpants	**un slip**
boxer shorts	**un caleçon**
a raincoat	**un imperméable**
shoes	**les chaussures** (nfpl)
a sweater	**un pullover**
a skirt	**une jupe**
a culotte	**une jupe-culotte**
to wear a skirt	**porter une jupe**
to get dressed	**s'habiller**
to put on one's dress	**enfiler sa robe**
well dressed	**bien habillé/habillée**
a T-shirt	**un T-shirt**

Key Structures

ce doit être	it must be
ce doit être lui	it must be him
ce doit être la voiture de Susie	it must be Susie's car
ce n'est pas	it is not
ce n'est pas moi	it is not me
le même blouson que moi	the same jacket as me
la même robe que toi	the same dress as you
détester que + subjunctive	
je déteste qu'une autre fille soit habillée comme moi	I hate another girl wearing the same gear as me

oh Biron...
mon amour

fais-moi un gros
gros baiser

SILENCE JE REGARDE LE TOP

enfin j'avais laissé mon livre "Le
jardin des racines grecques"
dans la cuisine et ...

PAPA JE REGARDE LE TOP!

Agrippine, ta
pauvre grand-mère,
c'est affreux

MAMAN JE REGARDE LE TOP

...

pas maintenant,
je regarde le top

ah, c'est toi; salut
vieille cloche

rien de spécial, je regarde
vaguement le top

c'est complètement nul!

BRETECHER

Understanding the text

affreux/affreuse	(adj)	horrible
un **amour**	(nm)	love
un **baiser**	(nm)	kiss
faire (v[5]) **un baiser**		to give a kiss
une **cloche** ©	(nf)	clod
complètement	(adv)	completely
une **cuisine**	(nf)	kitchen
faire	(v[5])	to do
une **grand-mère**	(nf)	grandmother
grec/grecque	(adj)	Greek
gros/grosse	(adj)	big
un **jardin**	(nm)	garden
laisser	(v[1])	to leave
un **livre**	(nm)	book
maintenant	(adv)	now
nul/nulle ©	(adj)	pathetic
pauvre	(adj)	poor
une **racine**	(nf)	root
regarder	(v[1])	to watch
rien	(adv)	nothing
salut	(excl)	hello
un **silence**	(nm)	silence
spécial/spéciale	(adj)	special
vaguement	(adv)	vaguely
vieux/vieille	(adj)	old

Television

television	la télévision
a television set	un téléviseur, une télé
a programme	une émission
the news	les informations
TV news	le journal télévisé
the weather	la météo
a film	un film
a documentary	un documentaire
a talk show	un talk show
a game show	un jeu télévisé
a series	une série télévisée
a soap opera	un feuilleton
a children's programme	une émission pour enfants
a studio	un studio
a sitcom	une comédie
an advert	une pub
a recorded broadcast	une émission en différé
a live programme	une émission en direct
a rerun	une rediffusion
an aerial	une antenne
a satellite dish	une antenne parabolique
a channel	une chaîne
cable television	la télévison par câble, le câble
the remote control	la télécommande
the TV licence	la redevance télé
digital TV	la télé numérique
high definition TV	la télé haute définition
to be on air	être à l'antenne
I like to watch TV	j'aime regarder la télé
what's on TV today?	qu'est-ce qu'il y a à la télé aujourd'hui?
there's a music programme on this afternoon	il y a une émission musicale cet après-midi
the presenter is very nice	l'animateur est très sympathique
did you watch the documentary about lions?	est-ce que tu as regardé le documentaire sur les lions?
that series was filmed in Grenoble	ces émissions ont été tournées à Grenoble
my boyfriend was on TV yesterday	mon copain est passé à la télé hier
to turn on/off the TV	allumer/éteindre la télé
to turn up/down the volume	augmenter/baisser le son
to switch channels	changer de chaîne
to flick through the channels	zapper

Le Top 50 is a television programme similar to Top of the Pops

Key Structures

silence!	quiet!
rien de spécial	nothing special

PENSE À TON AVENIR

Understanding the text

ainsi (adv)	so
l'**avenir** (nm)	future
le **béton** (nm)	concrete
en **béton** ◎	strong
une **biche** (nf)	doe
bon/bonne (adj)	good
un **canard** (nm)	duck
une **chatte** (nf)	cat
un/une **chirurgien/chirurgienne** (nm/f)	surgeon
une **chose** (nf)	thing
d'abord	first
se **dévaluer** (v[1])	to become devalued
être (v[3]) **en train de se dévaluer**	to become devalued
dire (v[14])	to say
épouser (v[1])	to marry
une **erreur** (nf)	mistake
les **études** (nfpl)	studies
faire (v[5]) **de bonnes études**	to get a good education
un **exemple** (nm)	example
par exemple	for instance
facile (adj)	easy
faire (v[5])	to do
ferai	→ **faire**
une **fille** (nf)	girl
le **fric** ◎ (nm)	money
grave (adj)	serious
c'est pas grave	it doesn't matter
homéopathique (adj)	homeopathic
l'**horreur** (nf)	loathing
avoir (v[10]) **horreur de**	to hate
une **idée** (nf)	idea
joli/jolie (adj)	pretty
laisser (v[1])	to let
laisser (v[1]) **tomber**	to drop
larguer ◎ (v[1])	to chuck
la **littérature** (nf)	literature
un max ◎	a lot
moi (pron)	me
un **notaire** (nm)	solicitor
une **passion** (nf)	passion
payer (v[32])	to pay
penser à (v[1])	to think about
plus tard	later
un **poussin** (nm)	chick
une **profession** (nf)	profession
une **puce** (nf)	flea
le **sang** (nm)	blood
seul/seule (adj)	only
si (conj)	if
sûr/sûre (adj)	certain
tomber (v[1])	to fall
tragique (adj)	tragic
trop (adv)	too much
veux	→ **vouloir**
vouloir (v[19])	to want

⊠ Work

an accountant	**un/une comptable**
an actor	**un/une acteur/actrice**
a bank clerk	**un/une employé/employée de banque**
a boss	**un/une patron/patronne**
a businessman/businesswoman	**un/une homme/femme d'affaire**
a caretaker	**un/une concierge**
a dentist	**un/une dentiste**
a doctor	**un médecin**
a driver	**un/une conducteur/conductrice**
an engineer	**un technicien/une technicienne**
a farmer	**un fermier/une fermière**
a fire officer	**un pompier**
a hairdresser	**un/une coiffeur/coiffeuse**
a journalist	**un/une journaliste**
a mechanic	**un/une mécanicien/mécanicienne**
a musician	**un/une musicien/musicienne**
a nurse	**un/une infirmier/infirmière**
a pensioner	**un/une retraité/retraitée**
a petrol pump attendant	**un/une pompiste**
a pilot	**un pilote**
a plumber	**un plombier**
a postman	**un facteur**
a programmer	**un/une programmeur/programmeuse**
a shopkeeper	**un/une commerçant/commerçante**
a teacher	**un professeur**
a vet	**un vétérinaire**
a waiter/waitress	**un/une serveur/serveuse**
a worker	**un/une ouvrier/ouvrière**
a writer	**un écrivain**
to work in a bank	**travailler dans une banque**
a salary	**un salaire**
working hours	**les heures** (nfpl) **de travail**
to earn	**gagner**
permanent contract	**contrat** (nm) **à durée indéterminée**
fixed-term contract	**contrat** (nm) **à durée déterminée**

⊠ Key Structures

Terms of endearment all translate more or less the same: my pet or poppet.
ma biche
ma puce
mon poussin
mon canard
ma chatte

Professions: no article is used in French

je serai comptable	I shall be an accountant
elle est médecin	she's a doctor
ce que tu veux faire	what you want to do

PROJETS D'AVENIR

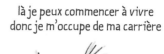

Understanding the text

après (adv)	afterwards
un **avenir** (nm)	future
avoir (v[10])	to have
une **carrière** (nf)	career
commencer (v[12])	to begin
complet/complète (adj)	complete, full
donc (conj)	therefore
émotionnel/émotionnelle (adj)	emotional
un/une **enfant** (nmf)	child
entre (prep)	between
faire (v[51])	to do
familial/familiale (adj)	family
gérer (v[26])	to manage
là (adv)	then
un **lifting** (nm)	face lift
un **nez** (nm)	nose
s'occuper de (v[1])	to take care of
opérer (v[26])	to operate on
un **pied** (nm)	foot
pouvoir (v[7])	to be able to
professionnel/professionnelle (adj)	professional
un **projet** (nm)	plan
quoi (pron)	what
refaire (v[51])	to redo
remodeler (v[46])	to remodel
retendre (v[6])	to tighten
une **réussite** (nf)	success
savoir (v[17])	to know
un **sein** (nm)	breast
une **tête** (nf)	head
un **ventre** (nm)	tummy
vivre (v[22])	to live

Key Structures

de la tête aux pieds	from top to toe
se faire opérer	to have surgery
se faire opérer des seins	to have a boob job
se faire refaire le nez	to have a nose job

NB In French when it is clear who owns the part of the body mentioned, no possessive determiner is used. See below for more examples.

The Human Body

a neck	un coup
a body	un corps
a back	un dos
a chest	une poitrine
an arm	un bras
a leg	une jambe
a bottom	un derrière
a waist	une taille
a hip	une hanche
a shoulder	une épaule
a knee	un genou
an elbow	un coude
a hand	une main
an ankle	une cheville
a foot	un pied
a toe	un orteil
a finger	un doigt
a heart	un cœur
a brain	un cerveau
a lung	un poumon
a stomach	un estomac
an ear	une oreille
an eye	un œil
eyes	les yeux
an eyebrow	un sourcil
an eyelash	un cil
an eyelid	une paupière
a cheek	une joue

a lip	une lèvre
hair	les cheveux (nmpl)

I go to the gym to keep fit	je vais au gymnase pour rester en forme
she has lost some weight	elle a maigri
I have a tummy/stomach-ache	j'ai mal au ventre
he has a headache	il a mal à la tête
I sprained my wrist	je me suis foulé le poignet
to have one's legs waxed	se faire épiler les jambes

BARBECUE

Understanding the text

un **agneau** (nm)	lamb
aller (v[25])	to go
amuser (v[1])	to make happy
attendre (v[6])	to wait for
avec (prep)	with
un **barbecue** (nm)	barbecue
bon (adv)	right
un **boulot** ⓖ (nm)	work
un **café** (nm)	café
aller (v[25]) **chercher**	to fetch
chez (prep)	at
compter sur (v[1])	to count on
conduire (v[47])	to drive
un/une **copain/copine** (nm/f)	boyfriend/girlfriend
une **côte** (nf)	chop
demander (v[1])	to ask
déposer (v[1])	to drop
espérer (v[26])	to hope
faire (v[5])	to do
un **franc** (nm)	franc
un **frigo** (nm)	fridge
à tout hasard	just in case
une **heure** (nf)	hour
s'inquiéter (v[26])	to worry
une **maman** (nf)	mum, mom
un **père** (nm)	father
un **pied** (nm)	foot
à pied	on foot
pile ⓖ (adv)	exactly
une **plage** (nf)	beach
un **poker** (nm)	poker
pourquoi (adv)	why
prendre (v[8])	to pick up
quand (conj)	when
quelqu'un (pron)	somebody
une **question** (nf)	question
pas question	no way
qui (pron)	who

ramener (v[36])	to drive back
un **rendez-vous** (nm)	appointment
rentrer de (v[1])	to go home from
un **retour** (nm)	journey back
revenir (v[18])	to come back
sinon (conj)	or else, otherwise
un **soir** (nm)	evening
le **stop** (nm)	hitching
faire (v[5]) **du stop**	to hitch
un **taxi** (nm)	taxi
va	→ aller
un **village** (nm)	village

⇥ Key Structures

il y a un barbecue	there's a barbecue
tu ne comptes pas sur moi pour	you don't bank on me to
aller vous chercher	pick you up
on demande à quelqu'un de nous ramener	we ask somebody to take us home
si ça t'amuse	if it makes you happy

⇥ Transport

a car	**une voiture**
a bus	**un bus**
a taxi	**un taxi**
the underground	**le métro**
a train	**un train**
a local train	**un train régional**
a boat	**un bateau**
a ferryboat	**un ferry**
a plane	**un avion**
a station	**une gare**
an airport	**un aéroport**
a bus stop	**un arrêt de bus**
a bicycle	**un vélo**
a moped	**une mobylette**
a motorcycle	**une moto**
a scooter	**un scooter**
they drove me to Oxford	**ils m'ont conduite à Oxford**
I'll drive there	**j'irai en voiture**
this train goes to Paris	**ce train va à Paris**
they came by boat	**ils sont venus en bateau**
the journey takes all night	**le voyage prend toute la nuit**
we're flying to London	**nous allons à Londres (en avion)**
to take a taxi	**prendre un taxi**
to change lines	**faire une correspondance**
to book a seat	**réserver une place**

SPORTS

Understanding the text

aller (v[25])	to go
alors (adv)	then
un **appartement** (nm)	flat, apartment
appeler (v[91])	to phone
un **ascenseur** (nm)	lift, elevator
avec (prep)	with
un **avocat** (nm)	lawyer
avoir (v[10])	to have
baby-sitter (v[1])	to babysit
en bas (adv)	downstairs
un **calme** (nm)	quiet
du calme!	calm down!
une **chaussure** (nf)	shoe
chaussures de sport	trainers
chercher (v[1])	to fetch
une **colère** (nf)	anger
se mettre (v[24]) **en colère**	to get angry
connaître (v[30])	to know
croire (v[44])	to believe
dès que (conj)	as soon as
descendre (v[6])	to go/come down(stairs)
dire à (v[141])	to tell
une **duchesse** (nf)	duchess
elle-même (pron)	herself
enfin (adv)	for heaven's sake
un **espace** (nm)	area
espace jeux	playground
un **étage** (nm)	floor, story
exagérer (v[26])	to exaggerate
faire (v[51])	to do
une **femme** (nf)	woman
un/une **gamin/gamine** ⓖ (nm/f)	kid
les **gens** (nmpl)	people
grand/grande (adj)	large
une **heure** (nf)	hour
hier (adv)	yesterday
un **immeuble** (nm)	building
mais (conj)	but
un/une **môme** ⓖ (nmf)	brat
monter (v[1])	to go/come up(stairs)
une **mort** (nf)	death
où (adv)	where
une **panne** (nf)	breakdown
en panne	out of order
payer (v[32])	to pay
peser (v[36])	to weigh
un **pied** (nm)	foot
à pied	on foot
pour (prep)	for
pourquoi (adv)	why
quand (conj)	when
qui (pron)	who
refuser (v[1])	to refuse
réparer (v[1])	to repair
répondre (v[6])	to answer
revenir (v[18])	to come back
savoir (v[17])	to know
tant pis (adv)	too bad
une **tarte** ⓖ (nf)	tart
une **tonne** (nf)	ton
tous (adj)	all

→ Sport

do you do any sports?	**vous faites du sport?**
which sport do you do?	**quel sport faites-vous?**
I go skiing	**je fais du ski**
I swim	**je nage**
soccer	**le football**
basket ball	**le basket**
tennis	**le tennis**
badminton	**le badminton**
swimming	**la natation**
running	**la course**
athletics	**l'athlétisme** (nm)
he plays football	**il joue au football**

The 16th arrondissement, **le seizième (arrondissement)** is a fashionable upmarket district in Paris.

→ Key Structures

j'avais mal aux pieds	my feet were aching
c'est quand même pas la mort!	it won't kill you!
c'est pas de la tarte!	it's no picnic!
refuser de payer	to refuse to pay

SUR ÉCOUTE

Understanding the text

aller (v[25])	to go
s'en aller	to leave
l' **argent** (nm)	money
argent de poche	pocket money
attendre (v[6])	to wait
aussi (adv)	too
avoir (v[10])	to have
un **bureau** (nm)	office
croire (v[44])	to believe
dire (v[14])	to say
embêter (v[1])	to annoy
énerver (v[1])	to get on [sb's] nerves
un **fait** (nm)	fact
en fait (nm)	in fact
un **franc** (nm)	franc
le **javanais** (nm)	→ note in bubble
se lever (v[36])	to stand up
une **mère** (nf)	mother
un **mois** (nm)	month
moyen/moyenne (adj)	average
pareil/pareille (adj)	identical
parler (v[1])	to talk
père (nm)	father
une **poche** (nf)	pocket
poser (v[1]) **des questions**	to ask questions
pouvoir (v[7])	to be able to, can
une **question** (nf)	question
quoi (pron)	what
rassied	→ se rasseoir
se rasseoir (v[48])	to sit down again
savoir (v[17])	to know
tout (pron)	everything
vouloir (v[19])	to want
zut! © (excl)	damn!

→ Economy

the budget	**le budget**
the economic situation	**la conjoncture économique**
the growth rate	**le taux de croissance**
market economy	**l'économie** (nf) **de marché**
macroeconomy	**la macro-économie**
foreign trade	**le commerce extérieur**
competition	**la concurrence**
consumption	**la consommation**
gross domestic product	**le produit intérieur brut**
gross national product	**le produit national brut**
public sector	**le secteur public**
private sector	**le secteur privé**
primary sector	**le secteur primaire**
secondary sector	**le secteur secondaire**
tertiary sector	**le secteur tertiaire**
a share	**une action**
the stock exchange	**la bourse**
the share index	**l'indice** (nm) **des valeurs boursières**
industry	**l'industrie** (nf)
heavy industry	**l'industrie lourde**
energy	**l'énergie** (nf)
agriculture	**l'agriculture** (nf)
tourism	**le tourisme**
unemployment	**le chômage**
business	**les affaires** (nfpl)
a company	**une entreprise**
supply	**l'offre** (nf)
demand	**la demande**
financial year	**l'exercice** (nm) **financier**
balance of trade	**la balance du commerce extérieur**
a balance sheet	**un bilan**
a price	**un prix**
the wholesale price	**le prix de gros**
the retail price	**le prix de détail**

javanais is a spoken slang formed by adding **av** in the middle of each syllable. **bonjour** would become **bavonjavour**.

→ Key Structures

je suis sur écoute	my phone is being tapped
dans le bureau c'est pareil	it's the same thing in the office
faire semblant	to pretend

LITTÉRATURE

Understanding the text

ah bon	really
s'appeler (v[9])	to be called
aucun/aucune (adj)	no
avec (prep)	with
banal/banale (adj)	unremarkable
pas banal/banale	unusual
bien (adj inv)	good
bien (adv)	well
combien (adv)	how many
combien de (det)	how many
complètement (adv)	completely
un/une **copain/copine** (nm/f)	friend
une **couverture** (nf)	cover
déjà (adv)	already
une **différence** (nf)	difference
différent/différente (adj)	different
donner (v[1])	to give
un **dos** (nm)	back
être (v[3])	to be
s'évanouir (v[41])	to faint
exactement (adv)	exactly
un **fait** (nm)	fact
une **femme** (nf)	woman
forcément (adv)	hardly surprising
fort/forte (adj)	strong
giga ⓖ (adj)	neat
il y a	there is, there are
illisible (adj)	unreadable
inférieur/inférieure (adj)	lower
jeune (adj)	young
le **jurassique** (nm)	Jurassic
un **livre** (nm)	book
lire (v[27])	to read
littérature (nf)	literature
lu	→ **lire**
moche ⓖ (adj)	ugly
moi (pron)	me
un **nom** (nm)	name
nul/nulle ⓖ (adj)	pathetic
où (adv)	where
à part	apart from
personne (pron)	nobody
pour (prep)	for
un **pourcentage** (nm)	percentage
premier/première (adj)	first
quand (conj)	when
quel/quelle (adj)	what
raconter (v[1])	to tell
un **résumé** (nm)	summary
rien (adv)	nothing
si (conj)	if
s'il vous plaît	please
une **suite** (nf)	sequel
des **toilettes** (nfpl)	toilets
très (adv)	very
trop ⓖ (adj)	incredible
TTC	tax included
tuer (v[1])	to kill
se vendre (v[6])	to sell
la **vie** (nf)	life
vieillir (v[41])	to age
vivre (v[22])	to live
votre (adj)	your

 Numbers

one	**un**
two	**deux**
three	**trois**
four	**quatre**
five	**cinq**
six	**six**
seven	**sept**
eight	**huit**
nine	**neuf**
ten	**dix**
eleven	**onze**
twelve	**douze**
thirteen	**treize**
fourteen	**quatorze**
fifteen	**quinze**
sixteen	**seize**
seventeen	**dix-sept**
eighteen	**dix-huit**
nineteen	**dix-neuf**
twenty	**vingt**
twenty-one	**vingt-et-un**
twenty-two	**vingt-deux**
twenty-three	**vingt-trois**
thirty	**trente**
forty	**quarante**
fifty	**cinquante**
sixty	**soixante**
seventy	**soixante-dix**
seventy-one	**soixante-et-onze**
eighty	**quatre-vingt**
eighty-one	**quatre-vingt-un**
ninety	**quatre-vingt-dix**
ninety-one	**quatre-vingt-onze**
hundred	**cent**
thousand	**mille**

When spelling double letters in French,
one says deux... .
deux r
deux p
un n ou deux?

 Key Structures

j'ai failli tomber raide	I nearly fainted
il a failli rater son train	he nearly missed his train
nous avons failli avoir un accident	we nearly had an accident

RENAISSANCE

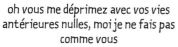

Understanding the text

d'abord	first
un **antérieur/antérieure** (adj)	previous
s'appeler (v[9])	to be called
avec (prep)	with
chinois/chinoise (adj)	Chinese
comment (adv)	how
cruel/cruelle (adj)	cruel
déprimer (v[1])	to depress
dire (v[14])	to say
un **droit** (nm)	right
avoir (v[10]) **le droit**	to have the right
dur/dure (adj)	hard
un/une **empereur/impératrice** (nm/f)	emperor/empress
ensuite (adv)	then
être (v[3])	to be
facile (adj)	easy
faire (v[5])	to do
inca (adj inv)	Inca
moi (pron)	me
le **monde** (nm)	people
tout le monde	everybody
naturellement (adv)	naturally
nul/nulle ⊚ (adj)	pathetic
parce que (conj)	because
personne (pron)	nobody
un **peuple** (nm)	people
peut-être (adv)	maybe
pouvoir (v[7])	to be able to
un/une **prince/princesse** (nm/f)	prince/princess
puissant/puissante (adj)	powerful
remonter à (v[1])	to date back to
une **renaissance** (nf)	rebirth
rien (adv)	nothing

un/une **roi/reine** (nm/f)	king/queen
savoir (v[17])	to know
un **siècle** (nm)	century
signaler (v[1])	to remind
très (adv)	very
trop (adv)	too much
la **vie** (nf)	life
vrai/vraie (adj)	true

→ Key Structures

qu'est-ce que tu en sais?	what do you know about it?
tout le monde ne peut pas	not everybody could be
avoir été Cléopâtre	Cleopatra
c'est comment?	what is it like?

→ Religion and Beliefs

Buddhist	**bouddhiste**
Christian	**chrétien/chrétienne**
Jewish	**juif/juive**
Muslim	**musulman/musulmane**
atheist	**athée**
agnostic	**agnostique**
believer	**croyant**
the Bible	**la bible**
the Koran	**le coran**
Catholic	**catholique**
Orthodox	**orthodoxe**
Protestant	**protestant**
to believe in God	**croire en Dieu**
to be an atheist	**être athée**
a church	**une église**
a temple	**un temple**
a mosque	**une mosquée**
a synagogue	**une synagogue**
a priest	**une prêtre**
a rabbi	**une rabin**

GLOSSARY

A

à cause de		because of	23
à côté de		next to	17
à part		apart from	65
à peu près		about	19
à pied		on foot	41, 59, 61
à plute ⊚		speak to you later	29
à tout hasard		just in case	59
aborder	(v[1])	to tackle	35
acheter	(v[31])	to buy	19, 33
acte	(nm)	action	49
admettre	(v[24])	to admit	33
affreux/affreuse	(adj)	horrible	53
Africain	(nm)	African	35
âge	(nm)	age	31
agneau	(nm)	lamb	59
agresser	(v[1])	to mug	41
ah bon		really	65
aimer	(v[1])	to love	33
ainsi	(adv)	so	55
aller	(v[25])	→ Key Structures	15, 31, 45;
		to be	27;
		to go	21, 23, 29, 37, 59, 61, 63
s'en aller		to leave	63
aller chercher	(v[25])	to fetch	59
allô!	(excl)	hello!	21
alors	(adv)	so	29, 33;
		then	11, 13, 25, 37, 45, 61
alors que	(conj)	even though	47;
		while	27
amant	(nm)	lover	15
amazonien/amazonienne	(adj)	Amazonian	47
américain/américaine	(adj)	American	29, 37
amitié	(nf)	friendship	33
amour	(nm)	love	15, 53
amoureux/amoureuse	(adj)	in love	33
amuser	(v[1])	to make happy	59
s'amuser	(v[1])	to enjoy oneself	15
an	(nm)	year	25, 29, 33
andouille ⊚	(nf)	fool	33
anglais	(nm)	English language	17
année	(nf)	year	19
anniversaire	(nm)	birthday	27, 45
antenne	(nf)	aerial	43
antenne parabolique	(nf)	satellite dish	43
antérieur/antérieure	(adj)	previous	49, 67
antibiotique	(nm)	antibiotic	35
anticiper	(v[1])	to anticipate	33
appartement	(nm)	flat, apartment	61
appel	(nm)	phone call	11
appeler	(v[9])	to phone	13, 35, 41, 61
s'appeler	(v[9])	to be called	65, 67
après	(adv)	afterwards	13, 57
arbre	(nm)	tree	45
arbre généalogique	(nm)	family tree	45
argent	(nm)	money	21, 39, 63
argent de poche		pocket money	63
arrêt	(nm)	stop	11
arrêter	(v[1])	to stop	39
arriver	(v[1])	to arrive	13, 23
ascenseur	(nm)	lift, elevator	61
Asie centrale	(nprf)	Central Asia	47
attendre	(v[6])	to wait (for)	11, 59, 63
au bercail ⊚		at home	37
au sujet de		about	15
aucun/aucune	(adj)	no	65
aujourd'hui	(adv)	today	19
aura		→ avoir	17
aussi	(adv)	also	49
		too	11, 21, 39, 45, 51, 63
autre	(adj)	other	9, 51
avaler	(v[1])	to swallow	49
avant	(prep)	before	13, 51
avec	(prep)	with	21, 31, 33, 35, 41, 59, 61, 65, 67
avenir	(nm)	future	15, 55, 57
avocat	(nm)	lawyer	61
avoir	(v[10])	to have	13, 17, 19, 21, 23, 31, 49, 57, 61, 63
avoir horreur de	(v[10])	to hate	21, 55
avoir le droit	(v[10])	to have the right	67
avoir peur	(v[10])	to be scared	15

B

baby-sitter	(v[1])	to babysit	43, 61
bagarre	(nf)	fight	13
baiser	(nm)	kiss	53
baisser	(v[1])	to go down	19
balance des paiements	(nf)	balance of payments	35
banal/banale	(adj)	unremarkable	65
barbecue	(nm)	barbecue	59
bavure	(nf)	blunder	47
BD	(nf)	cartoon strip	45
beau-père	(nm)	stepfather	23
beau/belle	(adj)	beautiful	29
beaucoup	(adv)	a lot	13
beauté	(nf)	beauty	11
belle		→ beau	29
belle jeune fille		beautiful young lady	29
ben! ⊚	(excl)	h'm!	11
béton	(nm)	concrete	55
biberon	(nm)	baby/nursing bottle	43
bîbîp		beep	35
biche	(nf)	doe	55
bien	(nm)	good	15
	(adj inv)	good	65
	(adv)	perfectly	37
		well	41, 65
bien sûr	(adv)	of course	23
bleu/bleue	(adj)	blue	25
bloquer	(v[1])	to block	11
blouson	(nm)	jacket	51
boire	(v[11])	to drink	13
bon	(adv)	right	15, 19, 29, 35, 59
bon/bonne	(adj)	good	55
bonbon	(nm)	sweet	43
boucler	(v[1])	to finish	45
bouillir	(v[40])	to boil	35
boulet	(nm)	millstone	15
boulot ⊚	(nm)	work	59
bouton	(nm)	button	11
bricole	(nf)	little something	31
bu		→ boire	13
bureau	(nm)	office	63
bus	(nm)	bus	39

C

c'est tout		that's all	43
ça	(pron)	that	29, 33
ça craint		it's the pits	17
ça suffit		that's enough	31
cadeau	(nm)	present	31
café	(nm)	café	59
Californie	(nprf)	California	37
calmant	(nm)	sedative	49
calme	(nm)	quiet	61
caméra	(nf)	cine-/movie camera	45
caméra vidéo	(nf)	camcorder	45
canard	(nm)	duck	55
caneton	(nm)	duckling	29
canon ⊚	(adj)	gorgeous	33
carrière	(nf)	career	57
carte	(nf)	card	45
carte d'identité	(nf)	identity card	13
cassé/cassée	(adj)	broken	21
casser	(v[1])	to break	21
casserole	(nf)	saucepan	13, 35
cassette	(nf)	cassette	17, 45
cassette vidéo	(nf)	video (cassette)	21
ce que		what	33
ce soir		tonight	43
ce/cette	(adj)	this	9

⊚ 68 ⊚

célébrité	(nf)	celebrity	11
celui-là	(pron)	that one	31
cervelle	(nf)	brain	19
cesser	(v[1])	to stop	15
cet		→ ce	9
chaîne	(nf)	chain	13
		channel	43
challenge	(nm)	challenge	29
chambre	(nf)	bedroom	49
chance	(nf)	chance	49
changer	(v[15])	to change	31
chanson	(nf)	song	45
chanter	(v[1])	to sing	17
chatte	(nf)	cat	55
chaud/chaude	(adj)	hot	21
chaussure	(nf)	shoe	61
chaussures de sport		trainers	61
chéri/chérie	(nm/f)	darling	27, 31
chez	(prep)	at	13, 41, 59;
		to	37
chinois/chinoise	(adj)	Chinese	67
chips	(nfpl)	crisps, potato chips	43
chirurgien/chirurgienne	(nm/f)	surgeon	55
choisir	(v[41])	to choose	47
chose	(nf)	thing	45, 55
cinéma	(nm)	cinema, movie theater	21, 27
classe	(nf)	class, classroom	35
cloche ◎	(nf)	clod	53
code	(nm)	code	39
		door code	23
coincer ◎	(v[12])	to catch	13
col roulé	(nm)	polo neck	51
colère	(nf)	anger	61
combien	(adv)	how many	65
		how much	43
combien de	(det)	how many	19, 65
comme	(conj)	like	51
commencer	(v[12])	to begin	57
comment	(adv)	how	19, 25, 27, 67
communication	(nf)	call	11
communiquer	(v[1])	to communicate	23
complainte	(nf)	lament	27
complet/complète	(adj)	complete, full	57
complètement	(adv)	completely	17, 53, 65
compliqué/compliquée	(adj)	complicated	35
comprendre	(v[8])	to understand	25, 33, 39
compte	(nm)	account	39
compter	(v[1])	to intend	37
compter sur	(v[1])	to count on	59
concert	(nm)	concert	25
conclure	(v[38])	to conclude	33
condition	(nf)	condition	45
conduire	(v[47])	to drive	59
confondre	(v[33])	to mix up, to mistake for	27
connaître	(v[30])	to know	17, 33, 61
contacter	(v[1])	to contact	23
content/contente	(adj)	satisfied	41
contexte	(nm)	context	25
continent	(nm)	continent	29
continuer	(v[1])	to continue	19, 25
contre	(prep)	against	49
contrôle	(nm)	test	43
copain/copine	(nm/f)	boyfriend/girlfriend	13
		friend	39, 43, 65
copie	(nf)	paper	47
copine	(nf)	→ copain	
cosmique	(adj)	cosmic	19
côte	(nf)	chop	59
couleur	(nf)	colour	45
coup	(nm)	job, trick	39
coup de fil ◎	(nm)	phone call	11, 27
coup de pied	(nm)	kick	25
courir après	(v[49])	to run after	39
cours	(nm)	class	17
cousin/cousine	(nm/f)	cousin	37
couverture	(nf)	cover	65
craindre ◎	(v[39])	to be a prat	33
crise	(nf)	crisis	19
croire	(v[44])	to believe	45, 51, 61, 63
cruel/cruelle	(adj)	cruel	67
cuisine	(nf)	kitchen	53
cul ◎	(nm)	bottom	33
cure	(nf)	course of treatment	29

cure de musées		lots of museum visits	29

D

d'abord		first	55, 67
d'accord		all right	25
d'ailleurs		besides	27, 33
de temps en temps		from time to time	49
décider	(v[1])	to make up one's mind	33
décision	(nf)	decision	29
dedans	(adv)	inside	45
dégoûter	(v[1])	to make [sb] sick	37
dégringoler	(v[1])	to slump	19
déjà	(adv)	already	25, 31, 65
demain	(adv)	tomorrow	17, 45
demander	(v[1])	to ask	11, 43, 59
demi-frère	(nm)	stepbrother	23, 45
demi-heure	(nf)	half an hour	39
dépendre	(v[6])	to depend	25
déposer	(v[1])	to drop	59
déprimer	(v[1])	to depress	67
depuis	(prep)	since	27, 29
déranger	(v[15])	to disturb	35
dernier/dernière	(adj)	last	19, 27
dès que	(conj)	as soon as	61
des tas de ◎		lots of	15
descendre	(v[6])	to go/come down(stairs)	61
dessin	(nm)	drawing	45
destin	(nm)	fate	49
déteindre	(v[13])	to run	13
déterminé/déterminée	(adj)	determined	49
détester	(v[1])	to hate	51
détour	(nm)	detour	29
deux	(num)	two	23, 39
se dévaluer	(v[1])	to become devalued	55
devenir	(v[18])	to become	49
deviner	(v[1])	to guess	19
devoir	(nm)	essay	17
devoir	(v[42])	to have to, must	41
différence	(nf)	difference	65
différent/différente	(adj)	different	65
dimanche	(nm)	Sunday	37
dire	(v[14])	to say	15, 25, 27, 29, 31, 33, 35, 49, 55, 63, 67
dire à	(v[14])	to tell	13, 19, 33, 35, 41, 61
discrétion	(nf)	discretion	33
donc	(conj)	therefore	49, 57
donner	(v[1])	to give	31, 65
dormir	(v[4])	to sleep	41
dos	(nm)	back	65
droit	(nm)	right	67
drôle	(adj)	funny	37
du calme!		calm down!	61
du tout		at all	51
duchesse	(nf)	duchess	61
dur/dure	(adj)	hard	49, 67

E

eau	(nf)	water	35
échec	(nm)	failure	15
s'éclater ◎	(v[1])	to have a great time	33, 37
écouter	(v[1])	to listen	11, 35
		to listen to	9, 21, 29
écran	(nm)	screen	43
écrire	(v[35])	to write	45
effort	(nm)	effort	15
elle-même	(pron)	herself	61
embarquer ◎	(v[1])	to pick up	13
embêter	(v[1])	to annoy	63
s'embêter	(v[1])	to be bored	21
embrasser	(v[1])	to kiss	13, 33
s'embrasser	(v[1])	to kiss (one another)	19
émission	(nf)	programme	21
emménager	(v[15])	to move in	19
emmener	(v[36])	to take	27
émotionnel/émotionnelle	(adj)	emotional	57
empereur/impératrice	(nm/f)	emperor/empress	67
en bas	(adv)	downstairs	61
en béton ◎		strong	55

en fait		in fact	63
en ligne		on line	11
en panne		out of order	61
en tous cas		in any case	51
en train de		in the process of	39
encore	(adv)	again	33
		still	41
encore plus		even more	45
énerver	(v[1])	to get on [sb's] nerves	49, 63
enfant	(nmf)	child	15, 21, 31, 37, 57
enfermé/enfermée	(adj)	locked in	9
enfin	(adv)	for heaven's sake	61
enfin bon	(adv)	anyway	37
ennuyer	(v[20])	to bore	27
s'ennuyer	(v[20])	to be bored	15
enregistrer	(v[1])	to record	45
ensuite	(adv)	then	67
enterrement	(nm)	funeral	27
entre	(prep)	between	57
entrée	(nf)	entrance	39
enveloppe	(nf)	envelope	23
environ	(adv)	about	25
envoyer	(v[2])	to send	9, 35, 37, 45
épatant/épatante	(adj)	splendid	25
épluché/épluchée	(adj)	peeled	35
époque	(nf)	time	23, 45
épouser	(v[1])	to marry	55
erreur	(nf)	mistake	55
esclave	(nmf)	slave	39
espace	(nm)	complex	11
		area	61
espace jeux		playground	61
espérer	(v[26])	to hope	59
espionner	(v[1])	to spy on	41
essayer	(v[32])	to try	25, 41
étage	(nm)	floor, story	61
être	(v[3])	to be	9, 15, 17, 39, 51, 65, 67
être censé/censée	(v[3])	to be supposed	41
être en larmes	(v[3])	to be in tears	13
être en retard	(v[3])	to be late	39
être hospitalisé/hospitalisée	(v[3])	to be taken to hospital	35
être obligé/obligée	(v[3])	to have to	29
être privé/privée de sorties	(v[3])	to be grounded	41
être sur un coup ⓖ	(v[3])	to be onto something big	39
études	(nfpl)	studies	55
s'évanouir	(v[41])	to faint	65
évident/évidente	(adj)	obvious	23
éviter	(v[1])	to avoid	11
évolution	(nf)	evolution	47
exactement	(adv)	exactly	65
exagérer	(v[26])	to exaggerate	39, 61
s'excuser	(v[1])	to apologize	33
exemple	(nm)	example	49, 55
exister	(v[1])	to exist	9, 27
expliquer	(v[1])	to explain	33
exploration	(nf)	exploration	29

F

facile	(adj)	easy	23, 55, 67
faillir	(v[50])	→ Key Structures	65
faire	(v[5])	to do	11, 21, 23, 31, 33, 37, 41, 45, 49, 55, 57, 59, 61, 67
		to make	15, 31, 39
faire un baiser	(v[5])	to give a kiss	53
faire du bien	(v[5])	to do good	15
faire de bonnes études	(v[5])	to get a good education	55
faire la chaîne	(v[5])	to make a chain	13
faire du stop	(v[5])	to hitch	41, 59
se faire agresser	(v[5])	to be mugged	41
se faire du souci pour	(v[5])	to worry about	41
fait		→ faire	21
	(nm)	fact	63, 65
familial/familiale	(adj)	family	57
famille	(nf)	family	37
fasse		→ faire	31
fatigant/fatigante	(adj)	tiring	45
faux	(adv)	out of tune	17
faux/fausse	(adj)	wrong	11
faveur	(nf)	favour	11
fax	(nm)	fax machine	23
		fax message	23

femme	(nf)	wife	23
		woman	33, 61, 65
femme de ménage	(nf)	cleaner	49
ferai		→ faire	55
fesse	(nf)	buttock	15, 25
feu	(nm)	fire	13
fille	(nf)	girl	29, 51, 55
filmer	(v[1])	to film	45
fils	(nm)	son	27, 29, 31
finalement	(adv)	finally	13
flair	(nm)	flair	33
flic ⓖ	(nm)	cop	13
fois	(nf)	time	27
forcément	(adv)	hardly surprising	65
forêt	(nf)	forest	47
fort/forte	(adj)	strong	65
fossoyeur	(nm)	gravedigger	15
fou/folle	(adj)	mad, crazy	31, 45
franc	(nm)	franc	39, 59, 63
France	(nprf)	France	35
fréquentable	(adj)	respectable	29
frère	(nm)	brother	27
fric ⓖ	(nm)	money	55
frigo	(nm)	fridge	59
fringues ⓖ	(nfpl)	clothes, gear	51
fruit de la passion	(nm)	passion fruit	43
futur/future	(adj)	future	49

G

galère ⓖ	(nf)	hell	43
gamin/gamine ⓖ	(nm/f)	kid	61
garage	(nm)	garage	11
garçon	(nm)	boy	41
génial/géniale	(adj)	brilliant	25
genre	(nm)	sort	39
gens	(nmpl)	people	31, 61
gentil/gentille	(adj)	kind	31, 45
gérer	(v[26])	to manage	57
gifle	(nf)	slap in the face	17
giga ⓖ	(adj)	neat	25, 31, 33, 37, 43, 65
gigot	(nm)	leg of lamb	25
glace	(nf)	ice cream	43
goinfre	(nm)	greedy pig	13
grand/grande	(adj)	large	43, 45, 61
grand magasin	(nm)	department store	21
grand-mère	(nf)	grandmother	35, 53
grand-oncle	(nm)	great uncle	27
grandes vacances	(nfpl)	summer holiday/vacation	37
grave	(adj)	serious	11, 55
grec/grecque	(adj)	Greek	53
grenade lacrymogène	(nf)	tear gas grenade	13
gros/grosse	(adj)	big	33, 53

H

habillé/habillée	(adj)	dressed	51
habiter	(v[1])	to live	49
hasard	(nm)	chance	11
heure	(nf)	hour	23, 27, 35, 41, 59, 61
hier	(adv)	yesterday	61
homéopathique	(adj)	homeopathic	55
horreur	(nf)	loathing	21, 55
horrible	(adj)	horrid	15, 51
hyper ⓖ	(adv)	very	21

I

ici	(adv)	here	37
idée	(nf)	idea	55
il y a		there is, there are	19, 21, 39, 65
il y a eu		there was, there were	13
illisible	(adj)	unreadable	65
imaginer	(v[1])	to imagine	13, 33
immeuble	(nm)	building	61
important/importante	(adj)	important	11
inca	(adj inv)	Inca	67
inférieur/inférieure	(adj)	lower	65
injuste	(adj)	unfair	47

s'inquiéter	(v[26])	to worry	17, 59
inscrire dans	(v[35])	to fit into	25
s'inscrire dans	(v[35])	to fit into	25
insister	(v[1])	to insist	27
intention	(nf)	intention	33
interaction	(nf)	interaction	25
intéressant/intéressante	(adj)	interesting	39
invasion	(nf)	invasion	35
invité/invitée	(nm/f)	guest	37
inviter	(v[1])	to invite	27, 29

J

jamais	(adv)	never	15, 27, 35, 41
jardin	(nm)	garden	53
javanais	(nm)	→ note on	63
jean	(nm)	jeans	33
jeune	(adj)	young	15, 29, 33, 39, 65
jeunesse	(nf)	youth	15
joie	(nf)	joy	31
joindre	(v[34])	to join	23
joli/jolie	(adj)	pretty	55
jouer	(v[1])	to perform	45
		to play	21
jour	(nm)	day	29, 49
journal	(nm)	paper	13
journaux	(nmpl)	→ journal	13
juillet	(nm)	July	29
jurassique	(nm)	Jurassic	65

K

karma	(nm)	karma	49

L

là	(adv)	now	29, 45
		there	21, 41
		then	57
laid/laide	(adj)	ugly	29
laisser	(v[1])	to leave	31, 53
		to let	35, 55
laisser tomber	(v[1])	to drop	55
lampe halogène	(nf)	halogen lamp	13
larguer	(v[1])	to chuck	55
larme	(nf)	tear	13
se lasser de	(v[1])	to grow tired of	39
lave-vaisselle	(nm)	dishwasher	19
le mieux		the best	49
le moins possible		as little as possible	49
lequel/laquelle	(pron)	which one	25
les deux taxis		taxi both ways	43
leurre	(nm)	illusion	15
se lever	(v[36])	to stand up	63
lifting	(nm)	face lift	57
ligne	(nf)	line	11, 23
lire	(v[27])	to read	17, 65
littérature	(nf)	literature	55, 65
livre	(nm)	book	53, 65
loin	(adv)	far	21
loisir	(nm)	leisure	21
long/longue	(adj)	long	29
lu		→ lire	65
lui	(pron)	him	33
		him/her	35
lycée	(nm)	secondary school (15-18)	19

M

m'	(pron)	→ me	29, 33
m²	(nm)	m², square metre	19
magasin	(nm)	shop	21
magnétoscope	(nm)	video, VCR	21
maintenant	(adv)	now	29, 53
mais	(conj)	but	33, 41, 45, 47, 61
malade	(adj)	ill, sick	31, 35
maman	(nf)	mum, mom	25, 59
manger	(v[15])	to eat	13
manquer de	(v[1])	to be lacking in	33

marcher	(v[1])	to work	43
mari	(nm)	husband	45
marque	(nf)	make	19, 43
matériel	(nm)	equipment	45
maths	(nfpl)	maths	43
matin	(nm)	morning	17, 41
maudire	(v[45])	to curse	49
me	(pron)	me	27
mec ⑤	(nm)	guy	33
même	(adv)	even	23, 25, 33, 39
		same	51
ménage	(nm)	housework	13
menu	(nm)	menu	25
merci	(nm)	thank you	31
mère	(nf)	mother	19, 21, 27, 35, 45, 63
mettre	(v[24])	to put	23, 35, 47, 49
mettre le feu à	(v[24])	to set fire to	13
se mettre en colère	(v[24])	to get angry	61
mignon/mignonne	(adj)	cute	15
mille	(num)	thousand	25
miracle	(nm)	miracle	27
moche ⑤	(adj)	ugly	65
mode	(nf)	fashion	25
moi	(pron)	me	9, 17, 37, 39, 47, 49, 51, 55, 65, 67
moi-même	(pron)	myself	9
moins	(adv)	less	9
mois	(nm)	month	63
moitié	(nf)	half	19
môme ⑤	(nmf)	brat	43, 61
monde	(nm)	people	11, 67
		world	15
montage	(nm)	editing	45
monter	(v[1])	to go/come up (stairs)	61
mort	(nf)	death	61
Moscou	(nprm)	Moscow	33
mot	(nm)	word	25
motiver	(v[1])	to motivate	37
mourir	(v[21])	to die	15
moyen/moyenne	(adj)	average	63
musée	(nm)	museum	29

N

n'importe quoi		anything	43
nature	(nf)	nature	29
naturel/naturelle	(adj)	natural	47
naturellement	(adv)	naturally	29, 67
ne ... plus	(adv)	no longer	25, 29
ne ... que	(adv)	only	25
neuf/neuve	(adj)	new	11
nez	(nm)	nose	57
nom	(nm)	name	19, 65
non	(adv)	no	21
notaire	(nm)	solicitor	55
nous	(pron)	us	13, 29
novembre	(nm)	November	27
nuit	(nf)	night	41
nul/nulle ⑤	(adj)	pathetic	21, 33, 43, 49, 53, 65, 67
numéro	(nm)	number	11, 23
numéro d'appel	(nm)	pager	23

O

obligatoire	(adj)	compulsory	29
obligé/obligée	(adj)	obliged	11
occasion	(nf)	second-hand car	11
occupé/occupée	(adj)	busy	21, 23
s'occuper de	(v[1])	to take care of	57
octobre	(nm)	October	27
oiseau	(nm)	bird	19
on	(pron)	we	17, 21, 33
oncle	(nm)	uncle	19
opérer	(v[26])	to operate on	57
où	(adv)	where	41, 61, 65
oublier	(v[28])	to forget	17, 31, 43
oui	(adv)	yes	37
ourlet	(nm)	hem	11

P

paire	(nf)	pair	33
palais	(nm)	palace	49
panne	(nf)	breakdown	61
papa	(nm)	dad	31
Pâques		Easter	37
par exemple		for instance	55
par hasard		by chance	11
par moments		at times	33
parc	(nm)	park	27
parce que	(conj)	because	13, 41, 67
pareil/pareille	(adj)	identical	63
parents	(nmpl)	parents	13, 37
parfaitement	(adv)	absolutely	19
parfum	(nm)	flavour	43
parler	(v[11])	to speak	23
		to talk	9, 33, 63
parole	(nf)	word	17
parrainer	(v[11])	to sponsor	35
partir	(v[4])	to leave	13, 27
pas banal/banale		unusual	65
pas la peine		not worth it	31
pas question		no way	59
passer	(v[11])	to put through	11
		to put [sb] on	21
		to spend	41
		to transfer	39
		to pass	47
passion	(nf)	passion	55
patate ⊚	(nf)	spud	35
pauvre	(adj)	poor	53
payer	(v[32])	to pay	19, 43, 55, 61
pense-bête	(nm)	reminder	35
penser à	(v[11])	to think of	23
		to think about	31, 55
percer	(v[12])	to crack	39
père	(nm)	father	13, 27, 29, 35, 59, 63
personne	(pron)	nobody	9, 13, 65, 67
peser	(v[36])	to weigh	61
petit/petite	(adj)	short	27
		little, young	35
		little	45
peuple	(nm)	people	67
peur	(nf)	fear	15
peut		→ pouvoir	21, 31
peut-être	(adv)	maybe	37, 45, 67
peux		→ pouvoir	21, 29, 39, 41
photo	(nf)	photo	51
pièce	(nf)	part	11
		play	45
pièce détachée	(nf)	spare part	11
pied	(nm)	foot	41, 57, 59, 61
pile	(nf)	battery	49
pile ⊚	(adv)	exactly	59
plage	(nf)	beach	59
plaisir	(nm)	pleasure	45
plan	(nm)	plan	25
plier ⊚	(v[28])	to make [sb] laugh	39
plus	(adv)	more	13, 39, 43
plus tard		later	55
poche	(nf)	pocket	63
point	(nm)	full stop, period	41, 49
poker	(nm)	poker	59
pomper ⊚	(v[11])	to crib, to copy	47
portable	(nm)	mobile	35
poser une question	(v[11])	to ask a question	9
poser des questions	(v[11])	to ask questions	33, 63
poster	(v[11])	to post, to mail	23
pote ⊚	(nm)	mate, pal	29
pour	(prep)	for	17, 27, 31, 61, 65
pour ne pas		so as not	41
pourboire	(nm)	tip	31
pourcentage	(nm)	percentage	65
pourquoi	(adv)	why	9, 13, 41, 59, 61
pourrais		→ pouvoir	31, 39
pourtant	(adv)	and yet	19
poussin	(nm)	chick	55
pouvoir	(v[7])	to be able to, can	11, 21, 29, 31, 39, 41, 45, 49, 57, 63, 67
préférer	(v[26])	to prefer	43
premier/première	(adj)	first	35, 47, 65
prendre	(v[8])	to take	11, 19, 29, 39, 45
		to pick up	59

près de	(prep)	near	19
pressing	(nm)	dry-cleaning	11
prévoir	(v[16])	to plan	13
prince/princesse	(nm/f)	prince/princess	67
pris		→ prendre	29
prix	(nm)	price	19, 31
problème	(nm)	problem	27
prochain/prochaine	(adj)	next	41
profession	(nf)	profession	55
professionnel/professionnelle	(adj)	professional	57
projet	(nm)	plan	37, 57
proposer	(v[11])	to offer	35
prude	(adj)	prudish	33
puce	(nf)	flea	55
puer	(v[11])	to stink	17
puisque	(conj)	since	41
puissant/puissante	(adj)	powerful	67

Q

quand	(conj)	when	17, 31, 33, 37, 39, 59, 61, 65
quart	(nm)	quarter	35
quel/quelle	(adj)	which	65
quelqu'un	(pron)	somebody	13, 23, 59
quelque chose		something	45
quelque part		somewhere	9
qu'est-ce qu'on fait?		what shall we do?	21
qu'est-ce que		what	27, 33, 41
question	(nf)	question	9, 37, 59, 63
qui	(pron)	who	9, 29, 31, 41, 59, 61
quoi	(pron)	what	17, 21, 23, 25, 37, 49, 57, 63

R

racine	(nf)	root	53
raconter	(v[11])	to tell	65
radin/radine ⊚	(adj)	stingy	31
ramener	(v[36])	to drive back	27, 59
ranch	(nm)	ranch	29
ranger	(v[15])	to tidy up	13, 49
rappeler	(v[9])	to phone back	29
se rasseoir	(v[48])	to sit down again	63
recevoir	(v[43])	to get	43
reconnaître	(v[30])	recognize	51
refaire	(v[5])	to do again	51
		to redo	57
refuser	(v[11])	to refuse	61
regarder	(v[11])	to watch	21, 53
regretter	(v[11])	to regret	11
remarquer	(v[11])	to notice	31
remodeler	(v[46])	to remodel	57
remonter à	(v[11])	to date back to	67
remuscler	(v[11])	to become muscular again	15
renaissance	(nf)	rebirth	67
rencontrer	(v[11])	to meet	15
rendez-vous	(nm)	appointment	35
		meeting	59
rendre malade	(v[6])	to make [sb] sick	31
rentrer	(v[11])	to come home	13, 41
rentrer de	(v[11])	to go home from	59
renverser	(v[11])	to knock over	13
réparer	(v[11])	to repair	61
repas	(nm)	meal	45
répéter	(v[26])	to repeat	33, 35
répondre	(v[6])	to answer	61
réseau	(nm)	network	39
ressource	(nf)	resource	47
rester	(v[11])	to stay	21
résumé	(nm)	summary	65
retard	(nm)	delay	39
retendre	(v[6])	to tighten	57
retour	(nm)	journey back	59
se retourner	(v[11])	to turn around	49
retrouver	(v[11])	to find (sth that was lost)	35
réussir	(v[41])	to succeed	39
réussite	(nf)	success	57
réveiller	(v[11])	to wake up	41
revenir	(v[18])	to come back	59, 61

rêver	(v[1])	to dream	39
réviser	(v[1])	to revise	13
rien	(adv)	nothing	21, 33, 53, 65, 67
roi/reine	(nm/f)	king/queen	67
rompre	(v[33])	to break up	19
rue	(nf)	street	41

S

sais		→ savoir	25
salle de bains	(nf)	bathroom	9
salut!	(excl)	bye!	11
		hello!	53
sang	(nm)	blood	55
sans arrêt		non-stop	11
saucisson	(nm)	pork sausage	43
sauf	(prep)	except	9, 13
sauf que	(conj)	except that	49
sauter	(v[1])	to jump	45
savoir	(v[17])	to know	13, 19, 23, 25, 37, 41, 57, 61, 63, 67
scénario	(nm)	scenario	39
scène	(nf)	scene	13
second/seconde	(adj)	second	47
sein	(nm)	breast	57
sel	(nm)	salt	35
semaine	(nf)	week	29, 45
se sentir	(v[4])	to feel	9
serrurerie	(nf)	locksmith's	11
se servir de	(v[4])	to use	43
seul/seule	(adj)	on one's own	15
		only	9, 55
si	(conj)	if	9, 45, 55, 65
siècle	(nm)	century	67
signal	(nm)	signal	9
signaler	(v[1])	to remind	67
silence	(nm)	silence	53
s'il vous plaît		please	65
simplement	(adv)	simply	45
sinon	(conj)	or else, otherwise	59
six	(num)	six	39
sœur	(nf)	sister	35
soir	(nm)	evening	37, 43, 59
soirée	(nf)	party	13
solitude	(nf)	solitude	23
solution	(nf)	solution	25
somptueux/somptueuse	(adj)	sumptuous	49
sonner	(v[1])	to ring	11
sortie	(nf)	outing	41
sortir avec	(v[4])	to go out with	33
souci	(nm)	worry	41
se souvenir que	(v[18])	to remember that	27
spécial/spéciale	(adj)	special	53
star	(nf)	star	45
stop	(nm)	hitching	41, 59
studio	(nm)	studio flat/apartment	19
subitement	(adv)	suddenly	39
suffire	(v[37])	to be enough	31
se suicider	(v[1])	to commit suicide	13
suis		→ être	51
suite	(nf)	sequel	65
sujet	(nm)	subject	15, 47
sur	(prep)	about	17
sûr/sûre	(adj)	certain	55

T

t'	(pron)	→ te	33
ta	(adj)	→ ton	21
tact	(nm)	tact	33
se taire	(v[29])	to be quiet	17
tais-toi		→ se taire	17
tant pis	(adv)	too bad	61
tapis	(nm)	rug	13
tarte ⓒ	(nf)	tart	61
tas	(nm)	heap	15
taxi	(nm)	taxi	41, 43, 59
te	(pron)	you	29
télé ⓒ	(nf)	TV	21
téléphone	(nm)	telephone	23
téléphone portable	(nm)	mobile phone	35

téléphoner	(v[1])	to make a phone call	39
		to phone	41
tellement	(adv)	so (much)	31, 33
temps	(nm)	time	45
terrible	(adj)	dreadful	13
tête	(nf)	head	57
timbre	(nm)	stamp	23
toi	(pron)	you	9, 17, 27, 33
toilettes	(nfpl)	toilets	65
tomber	(v[1])	to fall	55
ton/ta	(adj)	your	31
tonne	(nf)	ton	61
tôt	(adv)	early	13
toujours	(adv)	always	27, 39
tous	(adj)	all	61
tout	(pron)	anything	25
	(pron)	everything	31, 39, 41, 43, 47, 49, 63
	(adj)	any	15
	(adj)	every	33
tout à fait	(adv)	completely	37
tout le monde		everybody	11, 13, 33, 41, 67
tragique	(adj)	tragic	55
transformation	(nf)	alteration	11
travail	(nm)	work	23
travailler	(v[1])	to work	15
travaux	(nmpl)	work	19
très	(adv)	very	65, 67
trois	(num)	three	23
se tromper	(v[1])	to be mistaken	11
trop ⓒ	(adj inv)	incredible	65
	(adv)	too much	11, 21, 31, 55, 67
trouver	(v[1])	to find	19, 33
TTC		tax included	65
tuer	(v[1])	to kill	19, 31, 33, 65

U

un max ⓒ		a lot	33, 55
un point c'est tout		that's final	49

V

va		→ aller	31, 59
vacances	(nfpl)	holiday, vacation	37
vaguement	(adv)	vaguely	53
se vendre	(v[6])	to sell	65
venir	(v[18])	to come	13, 27, 39
ventre	(nm)	tummy	57
veux		→ vouloir	31, 55
se vexer	(v[1])	to get upset	25, 51
vide	(adj)	empty	15
vidéo	(nf)	video (cassette)	43
vie	(nf)	life	15, 39, 45, 49, 65, 67
vieillir	(v[41])	to age	65
vieux/vieille	(adj)	old	53
village	(nm)	village	59
vivre	(v[22])	to live	15, 57, 65
voilà	(prep)	there you are	29, 31
voir	(v[23])	to see	15, 19, 25, 27, 35
voiture	(nf)	car	35
voler	(v[1])	to steal	35
votre	(adj)	your	65
voué/vouée à l'échec		doomed to failure	15
vouloir	(v[19])	to want	13, 27, 31, 41, 43, 49 55, 63
vous	(pron)	you	47
voyage	(nm)	journey	15
vraiment	(adv)	really	51

W, X, Y, Z

Weston	(nm)	Weston shoes	33
y	(pron)	there	29
zéro	(nm)	zero, naught	39
zut! ⓒ	(excl)	damn!	63

VERBS

1 parler

Present indicative		Imperfect indicative		Present subjunctive		
je	parle	je	parlais	(que)	je	parle
tu	parles	tu	parlais	(que)	tu	parles
il	parle	il	parlait	(qu')	il	parle
nous	parlons	nous	parlions	(que)	nous	parlions
vous	parlez	vous	parliez	(que)	vous	parliez
ils	parlent	ils	parlaient	(qu')	ils	parlent

Future indicative		Perfect indicative			Present conditional	
je	parlerai	j'	ai	parlé	je	parlerais
tu	parleras	tu	as	parlé	tu	parlerais
il	parlera	il	a	parlé	il	parlerait
nous	parlerons	elle	a	parlé	nous	parlerions
vous	parlerez	nous	avons	parlé	vous	parleriez
ils	parleront	vous	avez	parlé	ils	parleraient
		ils	ont	parlé		
		elles	ont	parlé	**Past participle**	
						parlé/parlée

2 envoyer

Present indicative		Imperfect indicative		Present subjunctive		
j'	envoie	j'	envoyais	(que)	j'	envoie
tu	envoies	tu	envoyais	(que)	tu	envoies
il	envoie	il	envoyait	(qu')	il	envoie
nous	envoyons	nous	envoyions	(que)	nous	envoyions
vous	envoyez	vous	envoyiez	(que)	vous	envoyiez
ils	envoient	ils	envoyaient	(qu')	ils	envoient

Future indicative		Perfect indicative			Present conditional	
j'	enverrai	j'	ai	envoyé	j'	enverrais
tu	enverras	tu	as	envoyé	tu	enverrais
il	enverra	il	a	envoyé	il	enverrait
nous	enverrons	elle	a	envoyé	nous	enverrions
vous	enverrez	nous	avons	envoyé	vous	enverriez
ils	enverront	vous	avez	envoyé	ils	enverraient
		ils	ont	envoyé		
		elles	ont	envoyé	**Past participle**	
						envoyé/envoyée

3 être

Present indicative		Imperfect indicative		Present subjunctive		
je	suis	j'	étais	(que)	je	sois
tu	es	tu	étais	(que)	tu	sois
il	est	il	était	(qu')	il	soit
nous	sommes	nous	étions	(que)	nous	soyons
vous	êtes	vous	étiez	(que)	vous	soyez
ils	sont	ils	étaient	(qu')	ils	soient

Future indicative		Perfect indicative			Present conditional	
je	serai	j'	ai	été	je	serais
tu	seras	tu	as	été	tu	serais
il	sera	il	a	été	il	serait
nous	serons	elle	a	été	nous	serions
vous	serez	nous	avons	été	vous	seriez
ils	seront	vous	avez	été	ils	seraient
		ils	ont	été		
		elles	ont	été	**Past participle**	
						été (invariable)

4 sentir

Present indicative		Imperfect indicative		Present subjunctive		
je	sens	je	sentais	(que)	je	sente
tu	sens	tu	sentais	(que)	tu	sentes
il	sent	il	sentait	(qu')	il	sente
nous	sentons	nous	sentions	(que)	nous	sentions
vous	sentez	vous	sentiez	(que)	vous	sentiez
ils	sentent	ils	sentaient	(qu')	ils	sentent

Future indicative		Perfect indicative			Present conditional	
je	sentirai	j'	ai	senti	je	sentirais
tu	sentiras	tu	as	senti	tu	sentirais
il	sentira	il	a	senti	il	sentirait
nous	sentirons	elle	a	senti	nous	sentirions
vous	sentirez	nous	avons	senti	vous	sentiriez
ils	sentiront	vous	avez	senti	ils	sentiraient
		ils	ont	senti		
		elles	ont	senti	**Past participle**	
						senti/sentie

5 faire

Present indicative		Imperfect indicative		Present subjunctive		
je	fais	je	faisais	(que)	je	fasse
tu	fais	tu	faisais	(que)	tu	fasses
il	fait	il	faisait	(qu')	il	fasse
nous	faisons	nous	faisions	(que)	nous	fassions
vous	faites	vous	faisiez	(que)	vous	fassiez
ils	font	ils	faisaient	(qu')	ils	fassent

Future indicative		Perfect indicative			Present conditional	
je	ferai	j'	ai	fait	je	ferais
tu	feras	tu	as	fait	tu	ferais
il	fera	il	a	fait	il	ferait
nous	ferons	elle	a	fait	nous	ferions
vous	ferez	nous	avons	fait	vous	feriez
ils	feront	vous	avez	fait	ils	feraient
		ils	ont	fait		
		elles	ont	fait	**Past participle**	
						fait/faite

6 attendre

Present indicative		Imperfect indicative		Present subjunctive		
j'	attends	j'	attendais	(que)	j'	attende
tu	attends	tu	attendais	(que)	tu	attendes
il	attend	il	attendait	(qu')	il	attende
nous	attendons	nous	attendions	(que)	nous	attendions
vous	attendez	vous	attendiez	(que)	vous	attendiez
ils	attendent	ils	attendaient	(qu')	ils	attendent

Future indicative		Perfect indicative			Present conditional	
j'	attendrai	j'	ai	attendu	j'	attendrais
tu	attendras	tu	as	attendu	tu	attendrais
il	attendra	il	a	attendu	il	attendrait
nous	attendrons	elle	a	attendu	nous	attendrions
vous	attendrez	nous	avons	attendu	vous	attendriez
ils	attendront	vous	avez	attendu	ils	attendraient
		ils	ont	attendu		
		elles	ont	attendu	**Past participle**	
						attendu/attendue

7 pouvoir

Present indicative		Imperfect indicative		Present subjunctive		
je	peux	je	pouvais	(que)	je	puisse
tu	peux	tu	pouvais	(que)	tu	puisses
il	peut	il	pouvait	(qu')	il	puisse
nous	pouvons	nous	pouvions	(que)	nous	puissions
vous	pouvez	vous	pouviez	(que)	vous	puissiez
ils	peuvent	ils	pouvaient	(qu')	ils	puissent

Future indicative		Perfect indicative			Present conditional	
je	pourrai	j'	ai	pu	je	pourrais
tu	pourras	tu	as	pu	tu	pourrais
il	pourra	il	a	pu	il	pourrait
nous	pourrons	elle	a	pu	nous	pourrions
vous	pourrez	nous	avons	pu	vous	pourriez
ils	pourront	vous	avez	pu	ils	pourraient
		ils	ont	pu		
		elles	ont	pu	**Past participle**	
						pu

8 prendre

Present indicative		Imperfect indicative		Present subjunctive		
je	prends	je	prenais	(que)	je	prenne
tu	prends	tu	prenais	(que)	tu	prennes
il	prend	il	prenait	(qu')	il	prenne
nous	prenons	nous	prenions	(que)	nous	prenions
vous	prenez	vous	preniez	(que)	vous	preniez
ils	prennent	ils	prenaient	(qu')	ils	prennent

Future indicative		Perfect indicative			Present conditional	
je	prendrai	j'	ai	pris	je	prendrais
tu	prendras	tu	as	pris	tu	prendrais
il	prendra	il	a	pris	il	prendrait
nous	prendrons	elle	a	pris	nous	prendrions
vous	prendrez	nous	avons	pris	vous	prendriez
ils	prendront	vous	avez	pris	ils	prendraient
		ils	ont	pris		
		elles	ont	pris	**Past participle**	
						pris/prise

9 appeler

Present indicative		Imperfect indicative		Present subjunctive		
j'	appelle	j'	appelais	(que)	j'	appelle
tu	appelles	tu	appelais	(que)	tu	appelles
il	appelle	il	appelait	(qu')	il	appelle
nous	appelons	nous	appelions	(que)	nous	appelions
vous	appelez	vous	appeliez	(que)	vous	appeliez
ils	appellent	ils	appelaient	(qu')	ils	appellent

Future indicative		Perfect indicative			Present conditional	
j'	appellerai	j'	ai	appelé	j'	appellerais
tu	appelleras	tu	as	appelé	tu	appellerais
il	appellera	il	a	appelé	il	appellerait
nous	appellerons	elle	a	appelé	nous	appellerions
vous	appellerez	nous	avons	appelé	vous	appelleriez
ils	appelleront	vous	avez	appelé	ils	appelleraient
		ils	ont	appelé		
		elles	ont	appelé	**Past participle**	
						appelé/appelée

10 avoir

Present indicative		Imperfect indicative		Present subjunctive		
j'	ai	j'	avais	(que)	j'	aie
tu	as	tu	avais	(que)	tu	aies
il	a	il	avait	(qu')	il	ait
nous	avons	nous	avions	(que)	nous	ayons
vous	avez	vous	aviez	(que)	vous	ayez
ils	ont	ils	avaient	(qu')	ils	aient

Future indicative		Perfect indicative			Present conditional	
j'	aurai	j'	ai	eu	j'	aurais
tu	auras	tu	as	eu	tu	aurais
il	aura	il	a	eu	il	aurait
nous	aurons	elle	a	eu	nous	aurions
vous	aurez	nous	avons	eu	vous	auriez
ils	auront	vous	avez	eu	ils	auraient
		ils	ont	eu		
		elles	ont	eu	**Past participle**	
						eu/eue

11 boire

Present indicative		Imperfect indicative		Present subjunctive		
je	bois	je	buvais	(que)	je	boive
tu	bois	tu	buvais	(que)	tu	boives
il	boit	il	buvait	(qu')	il	boive
nous	buvons	nous	buvions	(que)	nous	buvions
vous	buvez	vous	buviez	(que)	vous	buviez
ils	boivent	ils	buvaient	(qu')	ils	boivent

Future indicative		Perfect indicative			Present conditional	
je	boirai	j'	ai	bu	je	boirais
tu	boiras	tu	as	bu	tu	boirais
il	boira	il	a	bu	il	boirait
nous	boirons	elle	a	bu	nous	boirions
vous	boirez	nous	avons	bu	vous	boiriez
ils	boiront	vous	avez	bu	ils	boiraient
		ils	ont	bu		
		elles	ont	bu	**Past participle**	
						bu/bue

12 coincer

Present indicative		Imperfect indicative		Present subjunctive		
je	coince	je	coinçais	(que)	je	coince
tu	coinces	tu	coinçais	(que)	tu	coinces
il	coince	il	coinçait	(qu')	il	coince
nous	coinçons	nous	coincions	(que)	nous	coincions
vous	coincez	vous	coinciez	(que)	vous	coinciez
ils	coincent	ils	coinçaient	(qu')	ils	coincent

Future indicative		Perfect indicative			Present conditional	
je	coincerai	j'	ai	coincé	je	coincerais
tu	coinceras	tu	as	coincé	tu	coincerais
il	coincera	il	a	coincé	il	coincerait
nous	coincerons	elle	a	coincé	nous	coincerions
vous	coincerez	nous	avons	coincé	vous	coinceriez
ils	coinceront	vous	avez	coincé	ils	coinceraient
		ils	ont	coincé		
		elles	ont	coincé	**Past participle**	
						coincé/coincée

13 déteindre

Present indicative		Imperfect indicative		Present subjunctive		
je	déteins	je	déteignais	(que)	je	déteigne
tu	déteins	tu	déteignais	(que)	tu	déteignes
il	déteint	il	déteignait	(qu')	il	déteigne
nous	déteignons	nous	déteignions	(que)	nous	déteignions
vous	déteignez	vous	déteigniez	(que)	vous	déteigniez
ils	déteignent	ils	déteignaient	(qu')	ils	déteignent

Future indicative		Perfect indicative			Present conditional	
je	déteindrai	j'	ai	déteint	je	déteindrais
tu	déteindras	tu	as	déteint	tu	déteindrais
il	déteindra	il	a	déteint	il	déteindrait
nous	déteindrons	elle	a	déteint	nous	déteindrions
vous	déteindrez	nous	avons	déteint	vous	déteindriez
ils	déteindront	vous	avez	déteint	ils	déteindraient
		ils	ont	déteint		
		elles	ont	déteint	**Past participle**	
						déteint/déteinte

14 dire

Present indicative		Imperfect indicative		Present subjunctive		
je	dis	je	disais	(que)	je	dise
tu	dis	tu	disais	(que)	tu	dises
il	dit	il	disait	(qu')	il	dise
nous	disons	nous	disions	(que)	nous	disions
vous	dites	vous	disiez	(que)	vous	disiez
ils	disent	ils	disaient	(qu')	ils	disent

Future indicative		Perfect indicative			Present conditional	
je	dirai	j'	ai	dit	je	dirais
tu	diras	tu	as	dit	tu	dirais
il	dira	il	a	dit	il	dirait
nous	dirons	elle	a	dit	nous	dirions
vous	direz	nous	avons	dit	vous	diriez
ils	diront	vous	avez	dit	ils	diraient
		ils	ont	dit		
		elles	ont	dit	**Past participle**	
						dit/dite

15 manger

Present indicative		Imperfect indicative		Present subjunctive		
je	mange	je	mangeais	(que)	je	mange
tu	manges	tu	mangeais	(que)	tu	manges
il	mange	il	mangeait	(qu')	il	mange
nous	mangeons	nous	mangions	(que)	nous	mangions
vous	mangez	vous	mangiez	(que)	vous	mangiez
ils	mangent	ils	mangeaient	(qu')	ils	mangent

Future indicative		Perfect indicative			Present conditional	
je	mangerai	j'	ai	mangé	je	mangerais
tu	mangeras	tu	as	mangé	tu	mangerais
il	mangera	il	a	mangé	il	mangerait
nous	mangerons	elle	a	mangé	nous	mangerions
vous	mangerez	nous	avons	mangé	vous	mangeriez
ils	mangeront	vous	avez	mangé	ils	mangeraient
		ils	ont	mangé		
		elles	ont	mangé	**Past participle**	
						mangé/mangée

16 prévoir

Present indicative		Imperfect indicative		Present subjunctive		
je	prévois	je	prévoyais	(que)	je	prévoie
tu	prévois	tu	prévoyais	(que)	tu	prévoies
il	prévoit	il	prévoyait	(qu')	il	prévoie
nous	prévoyons	nous	prévoyions	(que)	nous	prévoyions
vous	prévoyez	vous	prévoyiez	(que)	vous	prévoyiez
ils	prévoient	ils	prévoyaient	(qu')	ils	prévoient

Future indicative		Perfect indicative			Present conditional	
je	prévoirai	j'	ai	prévu	je	prévoirais
tu	prévoiras	tu	as	prévu	tu	prévoirais
il	prévoira	il	a	prévu	il	prévoirait
nous	prévoirons	elle	a	prévu	nous	prévoirions
vous	prévoirez	nous	avons	prévu	vous	prévoiriez
ils	prévoiront	vous	avez	prévu	ils	prévoiraient
		ils	ont	prévu		
		elles	ont	prévu	**Past participle**	
						prévu/prévue

VERBS continued

17 savoir

Present indicative		Imperfect indicative			Present subjunctive		
je	sais	je	savais		(que)	je	sache
tu	sais	tu	savais		(que)	tu	saches
il	sait	il	savait		(qu')	il	sache
nous	savons	nous	savions		(que)	nous	sachions
vous	savez	vous	saviez		(que)	vous	sachiez
ils	savent	ils	savaient		(qu')	ils	sachent

Future indicative		Perfect indicative			Present conditional	
je	saurai	j'	ai	su	je	saurais
tu	sauras	tu	as	su	tu	saurais
il	saura	il	a	su	il	saurait
nous	saurons	elle	a	su	nous	saurions
vous	saurez	nous	avons	su	vous	sauriez
ils	sauront	vous	avez	su	ils	sauraient
		ils	ont	su		
		elles	ont	su	**Past participle**	
						su/sue

18 venir

Present indicative		Imperfect indicative			Present subjunctive		
je	viens	je	venais		(que)	je	vienne
tu	viens	tu	venais		(que)	tu	viennes
il	vient	il	venait		(qu')	il	vienne
nous	venons	nous	venions		(que)	nous	venions
vous	venez	vous	veniez		(que)	vous	veniez
ils	viennent	ils	venaient		(qu')	ils	viennent

Future indicative		Perfect indicative			Present conditional	
je	viendrai	je	suis	venu	je	viendrais
tu	viendras	tu	es	venu	tu	viendrais
il	viendra	il	est	venu	il	viendrait
nous	viendrons	elle	est	venue	nous	viendrions
vous	viendrez	nous	sommes	venus	vous	viendriez
ils	viendront	vous	êtes	venus	ils	viendraient
		ils	sont	venus		
		elles	sont	venues	**Past participle**	
						venu/venue

19 vouloir

Present indicative		Imperfect indicative			Present subjunctive		
je	veux	je	voulais		(que)	je	veuille
tu	veux	tu	voulais		(que)	tu	veuilles
il	veut	il	voulait		(qu')	il	veuille
nous	voulons	nous	voulions		(que)	nous	voulions
vous	voulez	vous	vouliez		(que)	vous	vouliez
ils	veulent	ils	voulaient		(qu')	ils	veuillent

Future indicative		Perfect indicative			Present conditional	
je	voudrai	j'	ai	voulu	je	voudrais
tu	voudras	tu	as	voulu	tu	voudrais
il	voudra	il	a	voulu	il	voudrait
nous	voudrons	elle	a	voulu	nous	voudrions
vous	voudrez	nous	avons	voulu	vous	voudriez
ils	voudront	vous	avez	voulu	ils	voudraient
		ils	ont	voulu		
		elles	ont	voulu	**Past participle**	
						voulu/voulue

20 ennuyer

Present indicative		Imperfect indicative			Present subjunctive		
j'	ennuie	j'	ennuyais		(que)	j'	ennuie
tu	ennuies	tu	ennuyais		(que)	tu	ennuies
il	ennuie	il	ennuyait		(qu')	il	ennuie
nous	ennuyons	nous	ennuyions		(que)	nous	ennuyions
vous	ennuyez	vous	ennuyiez		(que)	vous	ennuyiez
ils	ennuient	ils	ennuyaient		(qu')	ils	ennuient

Future indicative		Perfect indicative			Present conditional	
j'	ennuierai	j'	ai	ennuyé	j'	ennuierais
tu	ennuieras	tu	as	ennuyé	tu	ennuierais
il	ennuiera	il	a	ennuyé	il	ennuierait
nous	ennuierons	elle	a	ennuyé	nous	ennuierions
vous	ennuierez	nous	avons	ennuyé	vous	ennuieriez
ils	ennuieront	vous	avez	ennuyé	ils	ennuieraient
		ils	ont	ennuyé		
		elles	ont	ennuyé	**Past participle**	
						ennuyé/ennuyée

21 mourir

Present indicative		Imperfect indicative			Present subjunctive		
je	meurs	je	mourais		(que)	je	meure
tu	meurs	tu	mourais		(que)	tu	meures
il	meurt	il	mourait		(qu')	il	meure
nous	mourons	nous	mourions		(que)	nous	mourions
vous	mourez	vous	mouriez		(que)	vous	mouriez
ils	meurent	ils	mouraient		(qu')	ils	meurent

Future indicative		Perfect indicative			Present conditional	
je	mourrai	je	suis	mort	je	mourrais
tu	mourras	tu	es	mort	tu	mourrais
il	mourra	il	est	mort	il	mourrait
nous	mourrons	elle	est	morte	nous	mourrions
vous	mourrez	nous	sommes	morts	vous	mourriez
ils	mourront	vous	êtes	morts	ils	mourraient
		ils	sont	morts		
		elles	sont	mortes	**Past participle**	
						mort/morte

22 vivre

Present indicative		Imperfect indicative			Present subjunctive		
je	vis	je	vivais		(que)	je	vive
tu	vis	tu	vivais		(que)	tu	vives
il	vit	il	vivait		(qu')	il	vive
nous	vivons	nous	vivions		(que)	nous	vivions
vous	vivez	vous	viviez		(que)	vous	viviez
ils	vivent	ils	vivaient		(qu')	ils	vivent

Future indicative		Perfect indicative			Present conditional	
je	vivrai	j'	ai	vécu	je	vivrais
tu	vivras	tu	as	vécu	tu	vivrais
il	vivra	il	a	vécu	il	vivrait
nous	vivrons	elle	a	vécu	nous	vivrions
vous	vivrez	nous	avons	vécu	vous	vivriez
ils	vivront	vous	avez	vécu	ils	vivraient
		ils	ont	vécu		
		elles	ont	vécu	**Past participle**	
						vécu/vécue

23 voir

Present indicative		Imperfect indicative			Present subjunctive		
je	vois	je	voyais		(que)	je	voie
tu	vois	tu	voyais		(que)	tu	voies
il	voit	il	voyait		(qu')	il	voie
nous	voyons	nous	voyions		(que)	nous	voyions
vous	voyez	vous	voyiez		(que)	vous	voyiez
ils	voient	ils	voyaient		(qu')	ils	voient

Future indicative		Perfect indicative			Present conditional	
je	verrai	j'	ai	vu	je	verrais
tu	verras	tu	as	vu	tu	verrais
il	verra	il	a	vu	il	verrait
nous	verrons	elle	a	vu	nous	verrions
vous	verrez	nous	avons	vu	vous	verriez
ils	verront	vous	avez	vu	ils	verraient
		ils	ont	vu		
		elles	ont	vu	**Past participle**	
						vu/vue

24 mettre

Present indicative		Imperfect indicative			Present subjunctive		
je	mets	je	mettais		(que)	je	mette
tu	mets	tu	mettais		(que)	tu	mettes
il	met	il	mettait		(qu')	il	mette
nous	mettons	nous	mettions		(que)	nous	mettions
vous	mettez	vous	mettiez		(que)	vous	mettiez
ils	mettent	ils	mettaient		(qu')	ils	mettent

Future indicative		Perfect indicative			Present conditional	
je	mettrai	j'	ai	mis	je	mettrais
tu	mettras	tu	as	mis	tu	mettrais
il	mettra	il	a	mis	il	mettrait
nous	mettrons	elle	a	mis	nous	mettrions
vous	mettrez	nous	avons	mis	vous	mettriez
ils	mettront	vous	avez	mis	ils	mettraient
		ils	ont	mis		
		elles	ont	mis	**Past participle**	
						mis/mise

25 aller

Present indicative		Imperfect indicative		Present subjunctive		
je	vais	j'	allais	(que)	j'	aille
tu	vas	tu	allais	(que)	tu	ailles
il	va	il	allait	(qu')	il	aille
nous	allons	nous	allions	(que)	nous	allions
vous	allez	vous	alliez	(que)	vous	alliez
ils	vont	ils	allaient	(qu')	ils	aillent

Future indicative		Perfect indicative			Present conditional	
j'	irai	je	suis	allé	j'	irais
tu	iras	tu	es	allé	tu	irais
il	ira	il	est	allé	il	irait
nous	irons	elle	est	allée	nous	irions
vous	irez	nous	sommes	allés	vous	iriez
ils	iront	vous	êtes	allés	ils	iraient
		ils	sont	allés		
		elles	sont	allées	**Past participle**	
					allé/allée	

26 inquiéter

Present indicative		Imperfect indicative		Present subjunctive		
j'	inquiète	j'	inquiétais	(que)	j'	inquiète
tu	inquiètes	tu	inquiétais	(que)	tu	inquiètes
il	inquiète	il	inquiétait	(qu')	il	inquiète
nous	inquiétons	nous	inquiétions	(que)	nous	inquiétions
vous	inquiétez	vous	inquiétiez	(que)	vous	inquiétiez
ils	inquiètent	ils	inquiétaient	(qu')	ils	inquiètent

Future indicative		Perfect indicative			Present conditional	
j'	inquiéterai	j'	ai	inquiété	j'	inquiéterais
tu	inquiéteras	tu	as	inquiété	tu	inquiéterais
il	inquiétera	il	a	inquiété	il	inquiéterait
nous	inquiéterons	elle	a	inquiété	nous	inquiéterions
vous	inquiéterez	nous	avons	inquiété	vous	inquiéteriez
ils	inquiéteront	vous	avons	inquiété	ils	inquiéteraient
		ils	ont	inquiété		
		elles	ont	inquiété	**Past participle**	
					inquiété/inquiétée	

27 lire

Present indicative		Imperfect indicative		Present subjunctive		
je	lis	je	lisais	(que)	je	lise
tu	lis	tu	lisais	(que)	tu	lises
il	lit	il	lisait	(qu')	il	lise
nous	lisons	nous	lisions	(que)	nous	lisions
vous	lisez	vous	lisiez	(que)	vous	lisiez
ils	lisent	ils	lisaient	(qu')	ils	lisent

Future indicative		Perfect indicative			Present conditional	
je	lirai	j'	ai	lu	je	lirais
tu	liras	tu	as	lu	tu	lirais
il	lira	il	a	lu	il	lirait
nous	lirons	elle	a	lu	nous	lirions
vous	lirez	nous	avons	lu	vous	liriez
ils	liront	vous	avez	lu	ils	liraient
		ils	ont	lu		
		elles	ont	lu	**Past participle**	
					lu/lue	

28 oublier

Present indicative		Imperfect indicative		Present subjunctive		
j'	oublie	j'	oubliais	(que)	j'	oublie
tu	oublies	tu	oubliais	(que)	tu	oublies
il	oublie	il	oubliait	(qu')	il	oublie
nous	oublions	nous	oubliions	(que)	nous	oubliions
vous	oubliez	vous	oubliiez	(que)	vous	oubliiez
ils	oublient	ils	oubliaient	(qu')	ils	oublient

Future indicative		Perfect indicative			Present conditional	
j'	oublierai	j'	ai	oublié	j'	oublierais
tu	oublieras	tu	as	oublié	tu	oublierais
il	oubliera	il	a	oublié	il	oublierait
nous	oublierons	elle	a	oublié	nous	oublierions
vous	oublierez	nous	avons	oublié	vous	oublieriez
ils	oublieront	vous	avez	oublié	ils	oublieraient
		ils	ont	oublié		
		elles	ont	oublié	**Past participle**	
					oublié/oubliée	

29 taire

Present indicative		Imperfect indicative		Present subjunctive		
je	tais	je	taisais	(que)	je	taise
tu	tais	tu	taisais	(que)	tu	taises
il	tait	il	taisait	(qu')	il	taise
nous	taisons	nous	taisions	(que)	nous	taisions
vous	taisez	vous	taisiez	(que)	vous	taisiez
ils	taisent	ils	taisaient	(qu')	ils	taisent

Future indicative		Perfect indicative			Present conditional	
je	tairai	j'	ai	tu	je	tairais
tu	tairas	tu	as	tu	tu	tairais
il	taira	il	a	tu	il	tairait
nous	tairons	elle	a	tu	nous	tairions
vous	tairez	nous	avons	tu	vous	tairiez
ils	tairont	vous	avez	tu	ils	tairaient
		ils	ont	tu		
		elles	ont	tu	**Past participle**	
					tu/tue	

30 connaître

Present indicative		Imperfect indicative		Present subjunctive		
je	connais	je	connaissais	(que)	je	connaisse
tu	connais	tu	connaissais	(que)	tu	connaisses
il	connaît	il	connaissait	(qu')	il	connaisse
nous	connaissons	nous	connaissions	(que)	nous	connaissions
vous	connaissez	vous	connaissiez	(que)	vous	connaissiez
ils	connaissent	ils	connaissaient	(qu')	ils	connaissent

Future indicative		Perfect indicative			Present conditional	
je	connaîtrai	j'	ai	connu	je	connaîtrais
tu	connaîtras	tu	as	connu	tu	connaîtrais
il	connaîtra	il	a	connu	il	connaîtrait
nous	connaîtrons	elle	a	connu	nous	connaîtrions
vous	connaîtrez	nous	avons	connu	vous	connaîtriez
ils	connaîtront	vous	avez	connu	ils	connaîtraient
		ils	ont	connu		
		elles	ont	connu	**Past participle**	
					connu/connue	

31 acheter

Present indicative		Imperfect indicative		Present subjunctive		
j'	achète	j'	achetais	(que)	j'	achète
tu	achètes	tu	achetais	(que)	tu	achètes
il	achète	il	achetait	(qu')	il	achète
nous	achetons	nous	achetions	(que)	nous	achetions
vous	achetez	vous	achetiez	(que)	vous	achetiez
ils	achètent	ils	achetaient	(qu')	ils	achètent

Future indicative		Perfect indicative			Present conditional	
j'	achèterai	j'	ai	acheté	j'	achèterais
tu	achèteras	tu	as	acheté	tu	achèterais
il	achètera	il	a	acheté	il	achèterait
nous	achèterons	elle	a	acheté	nous	achèterions
vous	achèterez	nous	avons	acheté	vous	achèteriez
ils	achèteront	vous	avez	acheté	ils	achèteraient
		ils	ont	acheté		
		elles	ont	acheté	**Past participle**	
					acheté/achetée	

32 payer

Present indicative		Imperfect indicative		Present subjunctive		
je	paie	je	payais	(que)	je	paie
tu	paies	tu	payais	(que)	tu	paies
il	paie	il	payait	(qu')	il	paie
nous	payons	nous	payions	(que)	nous	payions
vous	payez	vous	payiez	(que)	vous	payiez
ils	paient	ils	payaient	(qu')	ils	paient

Future indicative		Perfect indicative			Present conditional	
je	paierai	j'	ai	payé	je	paierais
tu	paieras	tu	as	payé	tu	paierais
il	paiera	il	a	payé	il	paierait
nous	paierons	elle	a	payé	nous	paierions
vous	paierez	nous	avons	payé	vous	paieriez
ils	paieront	vous	avez	payé	ils	paieraient
		ils	ont	payé		
		elles	ont	payé	**Past participle**	
					payé/payée	

33 rompre

Present indicative		Imperfect indicative		Present subjunctive		
je	romps	je	rompais	(que)	je	rompe
tu	romps	tu	rompais	(que)	tu	rompes
il	rompt	il	rompait	(qu')	il	rompe
nous	rompons	nous	rompions	(que)	nous	rompions
vous	rompez	vous	rompiez	(que)	vous	rompiez
ils	rompent	ils	rompaient	(qu')	ils	rompent

Future indicative		Perfect indicative			Present conditional	
je	romprai	j'	ai	rompu	je	romprais
tu	rompras	tu	as	rompu	tu	romprais
il	rompra	il	a	rompu	il	romprait
nous	romprons	elle	a	rompu	nous	romprions
vous	romprez	nous	avons	rompu	vous	rompriez
ils	rompront	vous	avez	rompu	ils	rompraient
		ils	ont	rompu		
		elles	ont	rompu	**Past participle**	
						rompu/rompue

34 joindre

Present indicative		Imperfect indicative		Present subjunctive		
je	joins	je	joignais	(que)	je	joigne
tu	joins	tu	joignais	(que)	tu	joignes
il	joint	il	joignait	(qu')	il	joigne
nous	joignons	nous	joignions	(que)	nous	joignions
vous	joignez	vous	joigniez	(que)	vous	joigniez
ils	joignent	ils	joignaient	(qu')	ils	joignent

Future indicative		Perfect indicative			Present conditional	
je	joindrai	j'	ai	joint	je	joindrais
tu	joindras	tu	as	joint	tu	joindrais
il	joindra	il	a	joint	il	joindrait
nous	joindrons	elle	a	joint	nous	joindrions
vous	joindrez	nous	avons	joint	vous	joindriez
ils	joindront	vous	avez	joint	ils	joindraient
		ils	ont	joint		
		elles	ont	joint	**Past participle**	
						joint/jointe

35 inscrire

Present indicative		Imperfect indicative		Present subjunctive		
j'	inscris	j'	inscrivais	(que)	j'	inscrive
tu	inscris	tu	inscrivais	(que)	tu	inscrives
il	inscrit	il	inscrivait	(qu')	il	inscrive
nous	inscrivons	nous	inscrivions	(que)	nous	inscrivions
vous	inscrivez	vous	inscriviez	(que)	vous	inscriviez
ils	inscrivent	ils	inscrivaient	(qu')	ils	inscrivent

Future indicative		Perfect indicative			Present conditional	
j'	inscrirai	j'	ai	inscrit	j'	inscrirais
tu	inscriras	tu	as	inscrit	tu	inscrirais
il	inscrira	il	a	inscrit	il	inscrirait
nous	inscrirons	elle	a	inscrit	nous	inscririons
vous	inscrirez	nous	avons	inscrit	vous	inscririez
ils	inscriront	vous	avez	inscrit	ils	inscriraient
		ils	ont	inscrit		
		elles	ont	inscrit	**Past participle**	
						inscrit/inscrite

36 emmener

Present indicative		Imperfect indicative		Present subjunctive		
j'	emmène	j'	emmenais	(que)	j'	emmène
tu	emmènes	tu	emmenais	(que)	tu	emmènes
il	emmène	il	emmenait	(qu')	il	emmène
nous	emmenons	nous	emmenions	(que)	nous	emmenions
vous	emmenez	vous	emmeniez	(que)	vous	emmeniez
ils	emmènent	ils	emmenaient	(qu')	ils	emmènent

Future indicative		Perfect indicative			Present conditional	
j'	emmènerai	j'	ai	emmené	j'	emmènerais
tu	emmèneras	tu	as	emmené	tu	emmènerais
il	emmènera	il	a	emmené	il	emmènerait
nous	emmènerons	elle	a	emmené	nous	emmènerions
vous	emmènerez	nous	avons	emmené	vous	emmèneriez
ils	emmèneront	vous	avez	emmené	ils	emmèneraient
		ils	ont	emmené		
		elles	ont	emmené	**Past participle**	
						emmené/emmenée

37 suffire

Present indicative		Imperfect indicative		Present subjunctive		
je	suffis	je	suffisais	(que)	je	suffise
tu	suffis	tu	suffisais	(que)	tu	suffises
il	suffit	il	suffisait	(qu')	il	suffise
nous	suffisons	nous	suffisions	(que)	nous	suffisions
vous	suffisez	vous	suffisiez	(que)	vous	suffisiez
ils	suffisent	ils	suffisaient	(qu')	ils	suffisent

Future indicative		Perfect indicative			Present conditional	
je	suffirai	j'	ai	suffi	je	suffirais
tu	suffiras	tu	as	suffi	tu	suffirais
il	suffira	il	a	suffi	il	suffirait
nous	suffirons	elle	a	suffi	nous	suffirions
vous	suffirez	nous	avons	suffi	vous	suffiriez
ils	suffiront	vous	avez	suffi	ils	suffiraient
		ils	ont	suffi		
		elles	ont	suffi	**Past participle**	
						suffi

38 conclure

Present indicative		Imperfect indicative		Present subjunctive		
je	conclus	je	concluais	(que)	je	conclue
tu	conclus	tu	concluais	(que)	tu	conclues
il	conclut	il	concluait	(qu')	il	conclue
nous	concluons	nous	concluions	(que)	nous	concluions
vous	concluez	vous	concluiez	(que)	vous	concluiez
ils	concluent	ils	concluaient	(qu')	ils	concluent

Future indicative		Perfect indicative			Present conditional	
je	conclurai	j'	ai	conclu	je	conclurais
tu	concluras	tu	as	conclu	tu	conclurais
il	conclura	il	a	conclu	il	conclurait
nous	conclurons	elle	a	conclu	nous	conclurions
vous	conclurez	nous	avons	conclu	vous	concluriez
ils	concluront	vous	avez	conclu	ils	concluraient
		ils	ont	conclu		
		elles	ont	conclu	**Past participle**	
						conclu/conclue

39 craindre

Present indicative		Imperfect indicative		Present subjunctive		
je	crains	je	craignais	(que)	je	craigne
tu	crains	tu	craignais	(que)	tu	craignes
il	craint	il	craignait	(qu')	il	craigne
nous	craignons	nous	craignions	(que)	nous	craignions
vous	craignez	vous	craigniez	(que)	vous	craigniez
ils	craignent	ils	craignaient	(qu')	ils	craignent

Future indicative		Perfect indicative			Present conditional	
je	craindrai	j'	ai	craint	je	craindrais
tu	craindras	tu	as	craint	tu	craindrais
il	craindra	il	a	craint	il	craindrait
nous	craindrons	elle	a	craint	nous	craindrions
vous	craindrez	nous	avons	craint	vous	craindriez
ils	craindront	vous	avez	craint	ils	craindraient
		ils	ont	craint		
		elles	ont	craint	**Past participle**	
						craint/crainte

40 bouillir

Present indicative		Imperfect indicative		Present subjunctive		
je	bous	je	bouillais	(que)	je	bouille
tu	bous	tu	bouillais	(que)	tu	bouilles
il	bout	il	bouillait	(qu')	il	bouille
nous	bouillons	nous	bouillions	(que)	nous	bouillions
vous	bouillez	vous	bouilliez	(que)	vous	bouilliez
ils	bouillent	ils	bouillaient	(qu')	ils	bouillent

Future indicative		Perfect indicative			Present conditional	
je	bouillirai	j'	ai	bouilli	je	bouillirais
tu	bouilliras	tu	as	bouilli	tu	bouillirais
il	bouillira	il	a	bouilli	il	bouillirait
nous	bouillirons	elle	a	bouilli	nous	bouillirions
vous	bouillirez	nous	avons	bouilli	vous	bouilliriez
ils	bouilliront	vous	avez	bouilli	ils	bouilliraient
		ils	ont	bouilli		
		elles	ont	bouilli	**Past participle**	
						bouilli/bouillie

41 réussir

Present indicative		Imperfect indicative		Present subjunctive		
je	réussis	je	réussissais	(que)	je	réussisse
tu	réussis	tu	réussissais	(que)	tu	réussisses
il	réussit	il	réussissait	(qu')	il	réussisse
nous	réussissons	nous	réussissions	(que)	nous	réussissions
vous	réussissez	vous	réussissiez	(que)	vous	réussissiez
ils	réussissent	ils	réussissaient	(qu')	ils	réussissent

Future indicative		Perfect indicative			Present conditional	
je	réussirai	j'	ai	réussi	je	réussirais
tu	réussiras	tu	as	réussi	tu	réussirais
il	réussira	il	a	réussi	il	réussirait
nous	réussirons	elle	a	réussi	nous	réussirions
vous	réussirez	nous	avons	réussi	vous	réussiriez
ils	réussiront	vous	avez	réussi	ils	réussiraient
		ils	ont	réussi		
		elles	ont	réussi	**Past participle**	
					réussi/réussie	

42 devoir

Present indicative		Imperfect indicative		Present subjunctive		
je	dois	je	devais	(que)	je	doive
tu	dois	tu	devais	(que)	tu	doives
il	doit	il	devait	(qu')	il	doive
nous	devons	nous	devions	(que)	nous	devions
vous	devez	vous	deviez	(que)	vous	deviez
ils	doivent	ils	devaient	(qu')	ils	doivent

Future indicative		Perfect indicative			Present conditional	
je	devrai	j'	ai	dû	je	devrais
tu	devras	tu	as	dû	tu	devrais
il	devra	il	a	dû	il	devrais
nous	devrons	elle	a	dû	nous	devrions
vous	devrez	nous	avons	dû	vous	devriez
ils	devront	vous	avez	dû	ils	devraient
		ils	ont	dû		
		elles	ont	dû	**Past participle**	
					dû/due	

43 recevoir

Present indicative		Imperfect indicative		Present subjunctive		
je	reçois	je	recevais	(que)	je	reçoive
tu	reçois	tu	recevais	(que)	tu	reçoives
il	reçoit	il	recevait	(qu')	il	reçoive
nous	recevons	nous	recevions	(que)	nous	recevions
vous	recevez	vous	receviez	(que)	vous	receviez
ils	reçoivent	ils	recevaient	(qu')	ils	reçoivent

Future indicative		Perfect indicative			Present conditional	
je	recevrai	j'	ai	reçu	je	recevrais
tu	recevras	tu	as	reçu	tu	recevrais
il	recevra	il	a	reçu	il	recevrait
nous	recevrons	elle	a	reçu	nous	recevrions
vous	recevrez	nous	avons	reçu	vous	recevriez
ils	recevront	vous	avez	reçu	ils	recevraient
		ils	ont	reçu		
		elles	ont	reçu	**Past participle**	
					reçu/reçue	

44 croire

Present indicative		Imperfect indicative		Present subjunctive		
je	crois	je	croyais	(que)	je	croie
tu	crois	tu	croyais	(que)	tu	croies
il	croit	il	croyait	(qu')	il	croie
nous	croyons	nous	croyions	(que)	nous	croyions
vous	croyez	vous	croyiez	(que)	vous	croyiez
ils	croient	ils	croyaient	(qu')	ils	croient

Future indicative		Perfect indicative			Present conditional	
je	croirai	j'	ai	cru	je	croirais
tu	croiras	tu	as	cru	tu	croirais
il	croira	il	a	cru	il	croirait
nous	croirons	elle	a	cru	nous	croirions
vous	croirez	nous	avons	cru	vous	croiriez
ils	croiront	vous	avez	cru	ils	croiraient
		ils	ont	cru		
		elles	ont	cru	**Past participle**	
					cru/crue	

45 maudire

Present indicative		Imperfect indicative		Present subjunctive		
je	maudis	je	maudissais	(que)	je	maudisse
tu	maudis	tu	maudissais	(que)	tu	maudisses
il	maudit	il	maudissait	(qu')	il	maudisse
nous	maudissons	nous	maudissions	(que)	nous	maudissions
vous	maudissez	vous	maudissiez	(que)	vous	maudissiez
ils	maudissent	ils	maudissaient	(qu')	ils	maudissent

Future indicative		Perfect indicative			Present conditional	
je	maudirai	j'	ai	maudit	je	maudirais
tu	maudiras	tu	as	maudit	tu	maudirais
il	maudira	il	a	maudit	il	maudirait
nous	maudirons	elle	a	maudit	nous	maudirions
vous	maudirez	nous	avons	maudit	vous	maudiriez
ils	maudiront	vous	avez	maudit	ils	maudiraient
		ils	ont	maudit		
		elles	ont	maudit	**Past participle**	
					maudit/maudite	

46 remodeler

Present indicative		Imperfect indicative		Present subjunctive		
je	remodèle	je	remodelais	(que)	je	remodèle
tu	remodèles	tu	remodelais	(que)	tu	remodèles
il	remodèle	il	remodelait	(qu')	il	remodèle
nous	remodelons	nous	remodelions	(que)	nous	remodelions
vous	remodelez	vous	remodeliez	(que)	vous	remodeliez
ils	remodèlent	ils	remodelaient	(qu')	ils	remodèlent

Present conditional

Future indicative		Perfect indicative			Present conditional	
je	remodèlerai	j'	ai	remodelé	je	remodèlerais
tu	remodèleras	tu	as	remodelé	tu	remodèlerais
il	remodèlera	il	a	remodelé	il	remodèlerait
nous	remodèlerons	elle	a	remodelé	nous	remodèlerions
vous	remodèlerez	nous	avons	remodelé	vous	remodèleriez
ils	remodèleront	vous	avez	remodelé	ils	remodèleraient
		ils	ont	remodelé		
		elles	ont	remodelé	**Past participle**	
					remodelé/remodelée	

47 conduire

Present indicative		Imperfect indicative		Present subjunctive		
je	conduis	je	conduisais	(que)	je	conduise
tu	conduis	tu	conduisais	(que)	tu	conduises
il	conduit	il	conduisait	(qu')	il	conduise
nous	conduisons	nous	conduisions	(que)	nous	conduisions
vous	conduisez	vous	conduisiez	(que)	vous	conduisiez
ils	conduisent	ils	conduisaient	(qu')	ils	conduisent

Future indicative		Perfect indicative			Present conditional	
je	conduirai	j'	ai	conduit	je	conduirais
tu	conduiras	tu	as	conduit	tu	conduirais
il	conduira	il	a	conduit	il	conduirait
nous	conduirons	elle	a	conduit	nous	conduirions
vous	conduirez	nous	avons	conduit	vous	conduiriez
ils	conduiront	vous	avez	conduit	ils	conduiraient
		ils	ont	conduit		
		elles	ont	conduit	**Past participle**	
					conduit/conduite	

48 rasseoir

Present indicative		Imperfect indicative		Present subjunctive		
je	rassieds	je	rasseyais	(que)	je	rasseye
tu	rassieds	tu	rasseyais	(que)	tu	rasseyes
il	rassied	il	rasseyait	(qu')	il	rasseye
nous	rasseyons	nous	rasseyions	(que)	nous	rasseyions
vous	rasseyez	vous	rasseyiez	(que)	vous	rasseyiez
ils	rasseyent	ils	rasseyaient	(qu')	ils	rasseyent

Future indicative		Perfect indicative			Present conditional	
je	rassiérai	j'	ai	rassis	je	rassiérais
tu	rassiéras	tu	as	rassis	tu	rassiérais
il	rassiéra	il	a	rassis	il	rassiérait
nous	rassiérons	elle	a	rassis	nous	rassiérions
vous	rassiérez	nous	avons	rassis	vous	rassiériez
ils	rassiéront	vous	avez	rassis	ils	rassiéraient
		ils	ont	rassis		
		elles	ont	rassis	**Past participle**	
					rassis/rassise	

VERBS continued

49 courir

Present indicative		Imperfect indicative			Present subjunctive		
je	cours	je	courais		(que)	je	coure
tu	cours	tu	courais		(que)	tu	coures
il	court	il	courait		(qu')	il	coure
nous	courons	nous	courions		(que)	nous	courions
vous	courez	vous	couriez		(que)	vous	couriez
ils	courent	ils	couraient		(qu')	ils	courent

Future indicative		Perfect indicative			Present conditional	
je	courrai	j'	ai	couru	je	courrais
tu	courras	tu	as	couru	tu	courrais
il	courra	il	a	couru	il	courrait
nous	courrons	elle	a	couru	nous	courrions
vous	courrez	nous	avons	couru	vous	courriez
ils	courront	vous	avez	couru	ils	courraient
		ils	ont	couru		
		elles	ont	couru	**Past participle**	
						couru/courue

50 faillir

Perfect indicative		
j'	ai	failli
tu	as	failli
il	a	failli
elle	a	failli
nous	avons	failli
vous	avez	failli
ils	ont	failli
elles	ont	failli

Past participle
failli